The Father's *Only* View of You

Embracing How Heaven Sees You

Written by:
Dr. Lon and Laurie Stettler

Copyright Page

Hebrew and Greek terms referenced are from James Strong, *The New Strong's Exhaustive Concordance of the Bible* (Nashville, TN: Thomas Nelson Publishers, 1990)

ISBN: 979-8-9936478-2-1

TABLE OF CONTENTS

Dedication

This book is dedicated first to our Lord Jesus Christ, Who through the ministry of the Holy Spirit, opened our eyes to our 'real' identity in Christ. This revelation of our identity, and how to activate that identity, has truly revolutionized both how we view the Lord and view ourselves. What a liberating and victorious way to live!

I, Lon, dedicate this book to my wonderful wife, Laurie, my companion, confidant, and friend. Her support and encouragement has been invaluable in the writing of this book. graciously co-labors with me in the work of the ministry.

I, Laurie, thank you, Lon, for a lifetime of love, adventures, joy, encouragement, and family.

Dedication

Introduction

The Lord desires that you know how all of heaven views and knows you as a Christian. More specifically, all three members of the Godhead – the Father, the son Jesus, and the Holy Spirit want to open your eyes to how they view and know you. How they know you is very different than religion's idea of how you are known.

Have you ever wondered:

> *How does the Father* ***see*** *or view me? Jesus view me? Holy Spirit view me?*
>
> *What do They* ***think*** *of me?*
>
> *How do they* ***talk*** *to one another about me?*

All very provocative questions. Once you understand how all of heaven views you, you will be able to answer these questions very clearly.

Why this book? With so much misinformation in the media about our identity and gender roles, it's timely to counter these lies with how the Godhead really knows us. The Father wrote an entire destiny book about your life before you were born (Psalm 139:16). He does not make mistakes. Your destiny includes your gender, your identity, your purpose (thesis), when you would be born, and even the selection of your parents. The Father's destiny for you was placed in your DNA before you were even born. With all this in mind, it is important to know who you were created to be!

We hope you aspire to learn how all of heaven knows you. The Lord longs for you to know how the members of the Godhead view you. After all, through the finished work of Christ, you are re-created into the image of the Father's dear Son. They only have one view of you as one who is recreated in the image of Jesus.

Ultimately, the Lord desires that you become a mature son or daughter. The Father wants to say to you what He told Jesus at the Jordan River: "You are My beloved Son, in You I am well-pleased." Obviously, He was speaking these words over Jesus as a *beloved* Son, but He longs to speak these words over you! To be seen and known as a beloved son or daughter requires that you first understand how all of heaven knows you.

In the pages ahead, you will learn not only how the members of the Godhead know you but also how you can activate and embrace your true identity in Christ. In Section 1 entitled, *The Real "You,"* you will gain a clear understanding of who you are in Christ as a foundation so you can move on to maturity. In section 2, *The Role of Repentance,* you will learn what repentance means and how to win in the courtroom of heaven. In section 3, *The Role of Faith in God*, you will learn what biblical faith is and how to activate your true identity in Christ – the one and only real version of you. In Section 4, *Toward Maturity*, we will learn what the Bible means by become a mature son or daughter. Let's dive in and learn how you are really known in heaven and how you can embrace that understanding.

Section 1

The Real "You"

With the end-goal of being a beloved son or daughter in mind, let's first understand our identity in Christ. We invite you on a journey to understand how God views and knows you as a new creation in Christ based on the finished work of Christ at Calvary. This is the Father's one and only view of you.

Once you understand more clearly how you are known in heaven, it will be easier to develop a clear conscience with God and maintain an enduring faith in Him.

In this section, we will provide you with a revelation of who you are in Christ. This understanding of the Father's one and only view of you will make it easier to have a clear and untainted conscience before God and the world. Let's begin!

Chapter 1

One Version of You

We each have a picture in our mind's eye of how we see ourselves. How you perceive yourself is a lens or filter you use as you think about *you*. You have a version of you in your mind. In your journey as a Christian, you probably have learned that some of your perceptions are correct and others are not, which you learn to correct over time. Your view is shaped by experiences over time and the degree to which you have conformed your thinking to what is true about you in scripture.

The place we are going to begin is with your Father's perception of you. After all, He is the one who wrote your destiny in heaven before you were born. He is the one who looks through the lens of the finished work of Christ on Calvary.

Have you ever wondered:

> *How does the Father* ***see*** *or view me? Jesus view me? Holy Spirit view me?*
>
> *What do They* ***think*** *of me?*
>
> *How do They* ***talk*** *to one another about me?*
>
> *How do the angels of heaven* ***talk*** *about me?*

The answers to these provocative questions are found in scripture and form our starting point. One of the most important revelations from scripture in the New Testament is the understanding that the three members of the Godhead *only have one version of you in mind – a new man who is born of the Spirit and washed in Jesus' blood!*

The Father, the Son, and Holy Spirit do not see or have two versions of you – the old man and the new man. They do not have double vision. There is only one version of you – your new man -- living in Jesus and learning to be one with Him. While you may hold two versions of yourself –the old and new natures -- the Godhead does not. They only recognize and know you as a new man in Christ with a divine nature. It is the only version of you they know. They are not double-minded about you.

> There is only one version of you – your new man!

The Father sees you in Jesus. Your quality of life in Him is the same as what the Father enjoys with Jesus and Holy Spirit. You are a new creation walking in love with your God, and learning to live in fellowship with Christ. The Father loves you the way He loves Jesus. In fact, He sees Jesus in you. The Holy Spirit, your Helper, loves you the same way He loves the Father and Jesus.

Once you are born-again, the Godhead only sees and knows you as a new creation. You now carry the image of the Son. Jesus put a full layer of Himself -- His personhood and deity -- into you when you were born-again. You now have what we will call a *born-again* spirit. This is what each member of the Godhead sees every day and in every situation when they look at you. They are calling you into your real identity in Christ as a beloved son or daughter.

Hear the Father's words to you:

> *Beloved, We are not seeing two of you...the old man and the new man. We do not have double vision. There is only one of you living in Jesus and learning to be one with Him. We are not in two minds or versions about you. We only speak to your identity as a saint, never as a sinner. We only work on the new you. The old you is dead, so let it rest in peace.*

When Christ was raised from the dead, your old nature was left in the grave and was not resurrected. When Jesus was buried, He took your old nature with Him. When He was raised from the dead, He left your old nature behind in the grave; it was not resurrected. You were resurrected with a new nature in newness of life. The apostle Paul said this very clearly:

> *Therefore if anyone is in Christ, he is a new creature; the old things* [old nature] *passed away; behold, new things* [nature of Christ] *have come. Now all these things are from God. (*2 Corinthians 5:17-18a, bracket added)

This scripture describes a transaction of sorts. The old man was crucified and buried with Christ and the new man in you was raised to newness of life.

The Father only sees one version of you. He sees you only in Christ. God only deals with the new man in us, because Jesus put to death the old man on the cross and left it buried in the grave. Yes, the Father is aware of your old nature but pays no attention to it because it has been put to death and left buried in the grave.

> God only deals with the new man in us, because Jesus put to death the old man on the cross.

You may not know it but you are positionally co-identified with Christ. As Jesus was crucified, you are *co-crucified* with Him because of your close identity with Christ. As Jesus was buried, you are *co-buried* with Him. As Jesus was resurrected, you are *co-resurrected!* As Jesus ascended and was seated at the right hand of the Father in heavenly places, so too you are *co-ascended* and *co-seated* with Christ in heavenly places.[1]

Old Self: Rom. 6:6; Col. 3:9; Eph. 4:22 **New Self**: Col. 3:10; Eph. 4:24

CO-IDENTIFIED WITH CHRIST

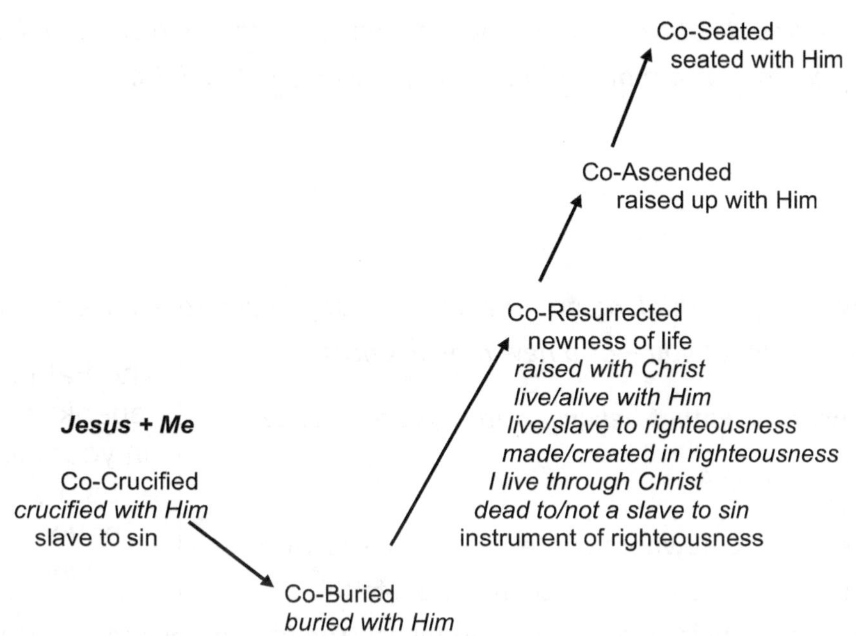

So, when Jesus Christ rose from the dead in newness of Life, none of your old nature was resurrected. It was left behind in the grave. Now the Father only sees the new you in Jesus. Hence, the title of this book: *the Father's only view of you*. The old you is dead.

[1] Here are the scriptural references for your further study. Co-Crucified: Gal. 2:20; Rom. 6:6. Co-Buried: Rom. 6:4; Col. 2:12. Co-Resurrected: Rom. 6:4, 8, 11; I Pet. 2:24; Col. 2:13; Eph. 2:4-5; Eph. 4:24. Co-Ascended: Eph. 2:4-6; Col. 3:1. Co-Seated: Eph. 2:6

Listen to the Father's words to you:

None of your old nature was resurrected. It was left behind in the grave.

When My beloved Son rose from the dead in newness of Life, none of your old nature made it through the resurrection. The old you is dead. It was left behind. We made sure of it.

When My Son died, so did you. He died for you and He died as you.

When He was buried, He took your old man with Him. When He was raised from the dead, He left your old nature behind. The old man can never be resurrected. It is gone, finished forever. Your new man is Christ in you, giving you His nature.

Let's Discuss!

How can you upgrade your thinking and speaking about yourself to align with the one version that God has about you – as a new man in Christ?

Do you believe what the Father believes and says about you?

The Father only speaks to you in your identity as a *saint*, never as a *sinner*.

When Jesus rose again to newness of life, who also rose with Him? You! His life, righteousness, grace, holiness, faith, character, and power all belong to you now in Jesus! The Father has redeemed you and recreated you in the image of His Son.

So the *real* you is your new nature, the nature of Jesus Christ living in you. Your *born-again spirit*[2] is as righteous, perfect, holy, and complete as Jesus. This is the only version of you that the Godhead sees and works with. Isn't this wonderful! (We will expand further on what's true about your redeemed spirit later in this book.) Now, the Father speaks to you in your identity as a *saint*, never as a *sinner*. The Godhead only works on the new you. The old you is dead so leave it alone.

---

[2] We use the term "born-again spirit" to mean the condition of your spirit after you receive Christ and are a new creation; it is our way of distinguishing it from the previous condition of your spirit (old nature, old man) that was spiritually dead.

God is inviting you to VIEW yourself, THINK about yourself, and TALK about yourself the same way that heaven does. You really cannot afford to think thoughts about yourself that God does not think about you. Likewise, you cannot afford to speak words about yourself that God has not said about you.

> You cannot afford to think thoughts about yourself that God does not think about you.

Your biggest battles are always about your true identity. Your adversary brings assaults against your sonship in Christ and against the Christ living in you. Your adversary does not want you to understand your true identity as you are striving to live from that true identity as a new creation. Your battles become more challenging when you do not clearly understand that, in the courts of heaven, *there is only one version of you – the new man.*

Your soul (especially your mind and conscience) must catch up with the transformation that has occurred in your spirit. If you are like most Christians, you have double-vision – that is, you see yourself as possessing both the old nature and the new nature at the same time. Why? Even though you know that you are a new creation in Christ, you still find yourself defaulting to the old nature and resurrecting your old nature. You still have memories and habits associated with your old nature that need to be replaced. So you live out two versions of yourself. Our goal through this book is to assist you in moving away from living out two versions of yourself and, instead, living out the one version of a new creation in Christ. It's what the Godhead sees and works on.

To catch up to your spirit, the soul part of you (in your mind and heart) must put off the old nature and put on the new nature. The apostle Paul explained this process when he wrote to the Ephesians and the Colossians.

> *. . .you lay aside the old self, which is being corrupted in accordance with the lusts of deceit, and that you be renewed in the spirit of your mind, and put on the new self, which in the likeness of God has been created in righteousness and holiness of the truth.* (Ephesians 4:22b – 24)

> *. . .since you laid aside the old self with its evil practices, and have put on the new self who is being renewed to a true knowledge according to the image of the One who created him.* (Colossians 3:9b-10)

In upcoming chapters we will share several tools to facilitate putting off the old nature and putting on the new one. The Father wants you to see the *real* you – the version of you that He sees because of the finished work of Christ. Understanding and living out of your new nature is essential to mastering the six principles of Christ and growing to maturity.

Let's Internalize and Apply!

1. The Father only has one view of you. What is that view?

   ____

   ____

2. Where is your old nature now?

   ____

   ____

3. Why does God only deal with the new man in us?

   ____

   ____

Chapter 2

Not Modifiable

One of the struggles we often have results from not making a clear distinction between our new nature and our old nature (the old man). The scripture is clear that God through the finished work of Christ put to death our old nature and raised us to newness of life in Christ. The Father knew that our old nature was not modifiable.

When Christ died for you, He killed off the old man because it was not modifiable.

Why did the Father kill off the old man at the cross? Because simply changing your old nature does not work. Father God knew that changing the 'old' you using *behavior modification* does not work. He already showed us that this does not work with the children of Israel consistently failing to modify their heart attitudes and behavior to keep the Law. Your old nature was not modifiable.

Instead, the Father gave you an entirely new nature (Greek: *anthropos* = new mankind) that has never existed before (Eph. 2:15)! Your new nature is the nature of Christ that is magnificent, majestic, supreme, and glorious. In your spirit, you are now a new creation that is remade in righteousness. The Father put you in Christ, and Christ into you, so He could treat you like He treats Jesus! You stand today before the Father as if you were Christ, because Christ stood before the Father as you.

The Father put you in Christ, and Christ into you, so He could treat you like He treats Jesus!

You now have permission to consider yourself dead to sin and alive unto Him. That is how the Father sees you.

> *Consider yourselves to be dead to sin, but alive to God in Christ Jesus.* Romans 6:11

Why should you consider yourself dead to sin? Because the Father does.

Holy Spirit will teach you the lifestyle of being alive in Him. So when God looks at you, He doesn't see anything wrong, because He killed off all sin and negativity. He's really happy about that now. He is not dealing with your sin because He already dealt with it once and for all (Rom. 6:10; Heb. 7:27; I Pet. 3:18). God does not and has not charged sin to any believer's account for over 2,000 years! Of course, you still will need to repent when the Spirit of God convicts you, but your sin issue was addressed two thousand years ago.

You are no longer a slave to sin. It is no longer your nature. The old nature is dead and at rest in the grave. God does not have a *sin conscious* view of you, because Jesus dealt with sin once and for all. Rather, the Godhead has a *righteousness conscious* view of you made in Their image and likeness. As we will learn, the Lord is working to remove a sin mindset about yourself and replace it with a righteousness mindset and understanding.

Unfortunately, most of us have been trying to resurrect our old nature for so long that we qualify as apostles. We are raising the dead every single day. We raise more corpses from the dead than all the apostles combined! We unknowingly attempt to resurrect our old nature – a dead corpse – as a default response.

You may find yourself asking:

> "I seem to always *default* to the old man rather than my new nature. I unknowingly respond from the flesh rather than from the Spirit. I'm learning Jesus killed off my old man at the cross and left it in the grave. How do I stop going directly to the old man and instead live only in my new nature?

Here's the thing: Even though your old nature was legally (in heaven's court) co-crucified and co-buried with Jesus, your old nature is still present in you. Your flesh nature (soul following the lead of your physical body) will default to it and resurrect it . . . if you allow it. We encourage you to consider yourself dead to sin and alive unto Him. Don't work on your sin; work on your righteousness, your true identity. That's what the Father is doing: upgrading your identity, not your sin.

> Don't work on your sin; work on your righteousness, your true identity.

Let's apply Luke 9:23-24 to what we are learning:

> *"If anyone wishes to come after Me, he must deny himself* [old nature], *and take up his cross daily and follow Me. For whoever wishes to save his life* [old nature] *will lose it, but whoever loses his life* [old nature] *for My sake, he is the one who will save it.* (brackets added)

Deny your old nature, do not default to it; rather, consider yourself dead to it and live free in Christ. Surrender your will to His will. Ask Jesus to fill you with the Holy Spirit so you display the fruit of the Spirit. Christ came to free you from the trappings of the old nature, so stay free in Christ!

As we continue through this book, you will learn ways to put off the old man so you can become the new man. For now, please know your new man is Christ in you, giving you His nature. Your new man has all the things you need to walk with God. It is built into Jesus, who is in you.

God is not practicing behavior modification on your old man in an attempt to upgrade your old nature. But religion is.

Religion is about trying to change the behavior of your old nature. But God is not practicing behavior modification on you. He is not upgrading your old nature. He already killed off your old man and placed it in the grave. Behavior modification does not work on a dead corpse.

> God is not calling out your behavior, He is calling you up into your identity in Christ.

God gave you a new Christ nature and now reprograms your mind with the mind of Christ so you reflect the ways of the new man rather than resort to habits of the old man. You do not become a new person by changing your behavior. You became the new man when you received Christ into your spirit.

God is not calling out your behavior, He is calling you up into your identity in Christ.

Each member of the Godhead always speaks to you according to your true identity in Christ. They only see one version of you. They see you as a *learner*, not a failure or a loser. Anything less would be an insult to the finished work of Christ.

> God only sees you as a *learner*, not a failure or a loser.

Let's Internalize and Apply!

1. The Father put you in Christ, and Christ in you, so that He could treat you like whom?

   ____

   ____

2. What happens in your life when you default to your old nature instead of the new man?

   ____

   ____

3. Why is the Godhead not practicing behavior modification on you?

____

____

4. T/F – God is always speaking to you from your identity in Christ.

Chapter 3

His Doing vs My Doing

So far you have learned that God has, sees, and knows only one version of you -- your new man. You have also learned that your old nature is not modifiable by religion or your efforts.

Still, through our church experience we feel the pressure to modify our old nature through our works or efforts. God changes our inside and works out, while we often try to change the outside to affect the inside. We confuse or blur *His Doing* versus *My Doing*. The scripture is clear that it is *"by* ***His doing*** *you are in Christ Jesus"* (I Cor. 1:30a).

Your adversary wants you to mix up your *being* with your *doing*. Because all your sins are completely forgiven (based on *His Doing*), there is nothing you can add (My Doing) to cause God to love and fully accept you more. Be watchful, for your adversary would like for you to think that it was, say, 90% *His Doing*, and 10% *My Doing*. No, it has always been *100% His Doing*.

Let's try to clarify biblically what our perspective should be.

Question: *Does the Father accept you?*

Answer: This is the wrong question. The real question should be: Is the Father satisfied with the finished work of Jesus? Ephesians 1:6 NKJV says you are *"accepted in the Beloved"*, and Romans 15:7 NASB states *"accept one another, just as Christ also accepted us to the glory of God."* So the answer is: To the *extent* that God the Father is *satisfied* with and accepts Jesus' finished work, He is *satisfied with me*! In my born-again spirit, it is 100% His doing, and 0% my doing.

My Doing	His Doing
0%	100%

The original question (*Does the Father accept you*?) puts the attention on *My Doing* when the real issue is on *His Doing* based on His finished work. Our adversary deceptively keeps trying to move our attention to the *My Doing* column rather than keeping it on the *His Doing* column, putting the attention on self rather than Jesus.

We must keep the focus on the *His Doing* side of the chart. Now, in your born-again spirit, the Father is 100% satisfied with you based on the finished work of Christ.

A few more examples:

Question: *Is God pleased with you?*

To the extent that God the Father is *fully pleased* with Jesus' finished work, He is *fully pleased with you*!

Question: *Are you holy?*

To the extent that *Jesus is holy* in the eyes of His Father, you are holy in the eyes of your heavenly Father in your born-again spirit. As a Christian, you first must *be* holy (I Pet. 1:16) in your born-again spirit, before you can *live* holy (I Pet. 1:15).

One final question: *Are you righteous?*

To the *extent that Jesus is righteous* in the eyes of His Father, you are righteous in the eyes of your Heavenly Father.

We hope you are learning the correct sentence stem to answer these questions: *To the extent that Jesus is _________ in the eyes of the Father, I am _______ in the eyes of my Father.*

As Jesus is NOW, so also are You in this World!

> . . .*as He is* [now], *so also are we* [in our born-again spirit] *in this world.* (I John 4:17, brackets added)

As Jesus Christ is *now*, so are you in your born-again spirit. Let that sink in. Your born-again spirit is—right now—as *perfect*, *mature*, and *complete* as Jesus Himself. Your born-again spirit is as perfect and complete as it'll ever be throughout all eternity. When God looks at you, He sees your born-again spirit that is as *righteous* and *holy* as Jesus.

To begin to see what has transpired in your born-again spirit, let's take a look at some of the truths about you.

As Jesus Christ is Now. . .		**So Am I in my Born-Again Spirit**
To the extent that Jesus is *righteous. . .*		I am *righteous* (Eph. 4:24; II Cor. 5:21)
To the extent that Jesus is *holy. . .*		I am *holy* (Eph. 4:24; I Cor. 3:17)
To the extent that Jesus is *totally accepted* by His Father. . .		I am *totally accepted* (Rom. 15:7) by my heavenly Father
To the extent that Jesus is *well pleasing* to His Father. . .		I am *well pleasing* to my Father (Matt. 3:17; Mark 1:11)
As Jesus now is *perfect, complete,* and *mature. . .*		I am *perfect, complete, and mature* (Heb. 10:14; 12:23)
As Jesus is *crowned with honor and glory. . .*		I am *crowned with honor and glory* (Heb. 2:7)
To the extent that Jesus was *approved* by His Father. . .		I am *approved* (I Thess. 2:4)
As Jesus was *chosen* by His Father. . .		I am *chosen* (Col. 3:12; I Peter 2:9)

Remember, we are looking at how God our heavenly Father is viewing you. When the Father looks at you in your born-again spirit, He sees Jesus! It's the only version of you that He recognizes and knows. The more you learn about who you are in your born-again spirit, the more you will discover about Jesus. Conversely, the more you learn about Jesus, the more you will discover about who you are in your spirit.

Let's Discuss!

Using the following sentence stem. . .

> *To the extent that Jesus is __________ in the eyes of the Father, I am ________ in the eyes of my Father.*

. . .what are three statements you can tell yourself when you need to flip the script in your mind and remind yourself of who God says you are?

Chapter 4

Jesus in the Mirror

You were created to look and be like God. The Psalmist said you are fearfully and wonderfully made.

> *Then God said, 'Let Us make man in Our image, according to Our likeness. . . God created man in His own image.* Genesis 1:26–27
>
> *. . .I am fearfully* [to stand in awe of] *and wonderfully made.* (Psalm 139:14b, brackets added)

You are *amazing*.

You are more *amazing* and *awesome* than you know.

Can you picture it? The Creator of the universe, who created you, takes a couple of steps back and looks at you and says, "Wow, you are awesome!" He stands in awe of you, His creation.

God *created* us, and now *recreated* us (you are now a 'new creation'), in such a way that we provide an accurate reflection of His glory back to Him and onto the world.

We invite you to look in God's mirror to see what He sees. You will look a whole lot like Jesus!

Each one of us is unique, and we were created to provide the most complete mirror image of God on earth. We are to reflect "Jesus in the Mirror!"

Identity Formation

Miles McPherson points out that we have two competing mirrors that we look at that affect our identity formation on the inside. There is a right mirror and a wrong mirror to view.[3]

---

[3] Miles McPherson, *God in the Mirror* (Grand Rapids, MI: Baker Publishing Group, 2013), 7-8, 13-32

The Right Mirror, God's Word. As a believer in Jesus, you now have an *I AM factor* from God – your individual uniqueness – which positions you above all living things to be in relationship with God. You look into your spiritual mirror, God's Word, to see who you are in your born-again spirit which looks like Jesus -- which Miles calls your *I AM factor*.

Your *I AM factor* reflects the *I AM-ness of God,* your 'God image'.

> *I am fearfully and wonderfully made.* Psalm 139:14
>
> *And You crown him with glory and majesty*! Psalm 8:5

A mistake is an event; it is not your identity!

Don't let anyone take your crown!

God has given you a new name – a "Christian". That new name reflects your I AM factor, the 'real you.' This new name has many facets which we will discover shortly.

Jesus, the Great I AM, has put His nature in our human spirit, and recreated our *I AM-ness*, the 'real me.'

The result is you will develop a 'righteousness consciousness' of yourself as you *own* the I Am-ness that you see in this spiritual mirror. You will see yourself as a *saint*, and not a *sinner.* A 'righteousness consciousness' is the gold standard you are to pursue.

The Wrong Mirror. The problem is we often have an inaccurate understanding of our new self as a Christian; we're not sure what is the 'real me'. Miles calls this inaccurate view our *I AM imposter.*

Your *I AM imposter* is an inaccurate or incomplete understanding of who you are as a Christian. It is a deception; a counterfeit version or knockoff of who God has created you to be.

In the natural your thoughts (about you) are not God's thoughts about you. For God's thoughts about you and me are higher than our natural thoughts. You must look into God's spiritual mirror to see what God thinks about you – how God created you and sees you.

Another way you develop this wrong understanding of yourself as a Christian is when you try to create a *name* for yourself separate from God – trying to create or find your significance, worth, and value, outside of God. Singer Frank Sinatra sang a famous song, *I Did It My Way*. Have you ever tried to create a name for yourself – apart from your relationship with God? How did that turn out?

Mistakes, Labels, and Lies

You are also looking in the wrong mirror when you think your identity is defined by the *mistakes* you've made, or the *labels* others have put on you, or the *lies* the Enemy has tried to put upon you. Together, these make up our I AM imposter.

Have you ever made a *mistake* like offended someone with your words; or yelled at your friend, spouse or child in anger; or did something disrespectful; or walked out on a relationship. A mistake is an event; it is not your *identity*! Refuse to be a prisoner of your past. A mistake is a life lesson, not a life sentence.

Or perhaps you have believed the *labels* that others have spoken over you: you're just average; or inferior; not capable; have an addiction; or you're a loser.

Maybe you have believed some of the *lies* the enemy has whispered in your ear, such as you don't have what it takes; you're not talented or special; you don't measure up.

And then there's the *negative self-talk* that doesn't let God get a Word in edgewise! If you don't silence those competing voices, they'll eventually deafen you. Which voice are you listening to?

A lie, a label, or a mistake can become the basis of the devil's accusation against you. Each of these are an assault against your sonship, your identity in Christ. However, when the enemy hears you assert your identity in Christ by rejecting those accusations, he no longer sees only you; he sees Jesus!

If you dwell on any of these falsehoods too long, you begin to believe them and identify with them, and you think of them as your name. When this happens, they create a wrong mental image on the inside. If you're not careful, the wrong image (from labels, mistakes, lies, negative self-talk) will become deeply entrenched emotionally in your heart and very difficult to overcome. A name is a powerful thing.

If you think any of these are your identity, you are looking in the *wrong* mirror. Continuing to look in the wrong mirror will result in you seeing yourself as a sinner, having a '*sin consciousness*'.

As a Christian, you are NOT

- what your *mistakes* say you are
- the *labels* people put upon you
- the *lies* the devil says about you

- who you've *tried to create* yourself to be

You *are who God says you are – deeply loved, completely forgiven, highly valued!*

What you may have done is not who you are. Your actions or wrong thinking do not define your identity in Christ. What God has said about you, and provided through Jesus Christ, defines your identity.

Let's Discuss!

What images do you have in your mind of who you are that are the result of looking in the wrong mirror – your mistakes?

Labels from others?

Lies of the enemy?

A name you've tried to create for yourself?

Your actions or wrong thinking do not define your identity in Christ. What God has said about you, and provided through Jesus Christ, defines your identity.

An Identity You Cannot Lose

Your God-given identity, which is in your born-again spirit, is something that you *cannot lose.* If something can be lost, then it is not your identity.

Too often we base our identity and self-worth on our:

- appearance
- talents and abilities
- smarts
- strength
- career success

But you can lose each one of these. Remember: *if you can lose it, it is not your real identity.*

Your God-given identity is based on *who God says you are* in the Bible, God's *spiritual mirror,* and not based on your appearance, or your talents/abilities, or your smarts, or your strength, or your successes.

You are who God says you are and you cannot lose it! The caveat is that you must live out the Christian life and ensure that you maintain your identify in Christ. Just as Adam and Eve forfeited their intimate relationship with God, so can you. Don't reject your great salvation resulting in your name being erased out of the Lamb's Book of Life (Rev. 3:5; Heb. 10:26, 29).

You were created to *wear the name* that you have been given – a name that reflects your I AM-ness from your Creator. Rather than make a name for yourself, wear the name that you have been given.

> *I have called you by name; you are Mine*! Isaiah 43:1
>
> *I will give him. . . a new name. . . I will write on him the name of My God. . .* Revelation 2:17; 3:12

Notice that God *exclusively* gets to name us, and not we ourselves or others (labels).

You not only bear God's image but you know His voice. Learning to hear the voice of God is key to discovering your destiny and fulfilling your potential. Know your true identity. When you know who you are, it doesn't matter who you are not. Don't focus on what you aren't, focus on what you are!

Is God's voice the *loudest* voice in your life?

That's the question.

If the answer is no, that's the problem.

Chronic noise may be the greatest impediment to your spiritual growth. When your life gets loud, with noise filling every frequency, you lose your sense of being. And when your schedule gets busy, you lose your sense of balance.

Pursue the truth about you which originates from your born-again spirit (which has access to the mind of Christ), and not from your natural mind. God's Word tells you what is true about your born-again spirit.

So where do you see yourself on the continuum below? Place an "X" on the continuum line below.

'I AM Factor' Continuum

I AM	I AM
Imposter____	Factor

Let's trade in your *I AM imposter* for your true *I AM factor*! Run toward your God-given destiny rather than away from it! Wear the name you have been given!

Let's Discuss!

How do you walk away from your "I AM imposter" so that you wear the name you've been given?

What image do you see in the mirror? Which mirror are you looking at – I AM imposter? Your God image?

How can you go from looking in the I AM imposter mirror (your mistakes, labels from others, lies from enemy) and flip the script so that you look more intently at your I AM factor – the 'real' you?

Let's Internalize and Apply!

1. What is meant by your "I AM factor"?

   ____

   ____

2. How does it differ from the "I AM imposter?"

   ____

   ____

3. How do you move from the "I AM imposter" to the "I AM factor?"

   ____

   ____

4. Have you ever tried to create a name for yourself – apart from your relationship with God -- trying to find significance, worth, and value separate from God? How did that turn out? Who has the exclusive right to give you a name? How should you respond?

Chapter 5

What's True about the One Version of You

But we have this treasure in earthen vessels. . . 2 Corinthians 4:7a

Since the Lord only sees and talks about one version of you as a new creation or a new man in Christ, it is instructive to learn a little more about what is true about this version of you.[4] Jesus is the Treasure who lives in you, so your born-again spirit is a "treasure" within you. Let's learn a little more about what's true about you as a new creation.

The spirit part of you was instantly and completely transformed when you were born-again. Let's drill down a little more and learn some key truths about your born-again spirit – the one version that the Father sees and talks about. After all, He is the one who recreated you through Christ Jesus so you probably want to learn more about what this means.

Truth #1: At this very moment, your born-again spirit is as perfect and complete as it'll ever be throughout all eternity.

Did you know that you are *perfect* and *complete* in your born-again spirit? The writer of Hebrews tells us that through the finished work of Christ, the spirit of the righteous are made *perfect* (Heb.12:23). Your born-again spirit is sealed to keep out the impurities and evil, and seal in your new nature -- which is righteous, holy, perfect, complete.[5] When you were born-again, your spirit was encased – vacuum packed – by the Holy Spirit for preservation. Your born-again spirit retains the holiness and purity of Christ – and will for eternity!

As a Christian, when you sin, that sin cannot enter into your spirit but it can have a negative impact on your soul and body. Sin, if left unconfessed, can have an oppressive effect on your soul and ultimately on your body. It will also weigh heavily upon your spirit and fellowship with God and with other people.

---

[4] See 2 Corinthians 5:17; Galatians 6:15; Ephesians 2:15

[5] See 2 Corinthians 5:21; Ephesians 4:24; Hebrews 12:23; Colossians 2:10

When you enter heaven, you will not get a new spirit upon your arrival there, nor will your spirit need to be matured, or completed, or cleansed. Your spirit (the "new" man) down here is as perfect and complete as it'll ever be throughout all eternity.

Truth #2: Your born-again spirit is—right now—as *perfect, mature*, and *complete* as Jesus Himself.

You are a born-again spirit, you have a soul, and you live in a body. You are a newly created person who did not exist before – a new kind of mankind that is – right now – as perfect, mature, and complete as Jesus Himself. This should not be surprising because you received the spirit of Christ, God's holy Son, into your spirit when you were born again. You are as perfect and complete as you will ever be throughout all eternity.

The Greek word for a new *man* in Ephesians 2:15 is *anthropos*, which means a new kind or race of man. You are now a member of a new race of people – the *saints* race, or the church race. You are part of a newly created people who did not exist before – a new superior kind of mankind now seated at the right hand of the Father. As a member of the saints race of people, you are superior to the first man, Adam. While Adam was created in innocence, you have been created in *righteousness*! And while Adam had authority and dominion over the earth, you have authority in *both* heaven and earth.

You are as clean, holy, and pure as Jesus himself in your born-again spirit. So continue to live in freedom and repent of anything that defiles your body and your soul.

> *. . . as He* [Jesus] *is* [now]*, so also are we in this world.* **(**I John 4:17, brackets mine)

Let's Discuss!

Your born-again spirit is as righteous, holy, perfect, and compete as Jesus. How difficult is it for you to believe that statement?

As Jesus is now, so also are you in your born-again spirit. What will you do to internalize and embrace this truth?

Unfortunately, you (should we say *we*) still have some "old data" from our "old nature" (wrong self-image, values, mannerisms) still lingering in our thinking, and we try to impose it upon our "new man" and it simply does not work. You must completely put off the old self with its memories and habits and reprogram your soul with the "new man" of your born-again spirit.

God's spiritual mirror, His Word, perfectly reflects your born-again spirit, the 'real' you, which looks a lot like Jesus!

Truth #3: When you sin, it does not originate from your born-again spirit. Your born-again spirit does NOT participate when you sin.

Your born-again spirit is *not* capable of committing sin. Read the following scriptures closely.

> *Whoever has been born of God does not sin, for His* [Christ's] *seed remains in him; and he cannot sin, because he has been born of God.* (I John 3:9, NKJV, bracket added)
>
> *We know that no one who is born of God sins; but He* [Christ] *who was born of God keeps him, and the evil one does not touch him.* (I John 5:18, bracket added)
>
> ". . .*as He* [Christ] is [now], *so also are we in this world.*" (I John 4:17)
>
> . . .*for God cannot be tempted by evil, and He Himself* [in your born-again spirit] *does not tempt anyone.* (James 1:13, brackets mine)

When your *soul (mind and will) agrees with your spirit,* you release and experience the *life* of God. The Christian life, by design, is intended to be a life of complete *dependence* on the Lord. When you follow the lead of your spirit, you release life, and not sin. This is where God wants us to live and walk. You live the crucified life (rejecting the flesh with its passions and desires) which enables you to walk in the Spirit, be led by the Spirit, and live in the Spirit. Said another way, when you walk in the Spirit, you will not carry out the desires of the flesh. You are walking in love, faith, wisdom, and as a child of Light. You are allowing your body to be the temple of the Holy Spirit that Christ wants it to be.[6]

When your *soul agrees with your spirit*, you release and experience the *life* of God.

[6] Galatians 2:20; 5:16, 18, 25; Ephesians 5:2, 8, 15; I Corinthians 6:19

However, when you choose to live *independent* of the Lord, your *soul agrees with your body* or flesh (apart from your spirit). This closes the valve of the supernatural flow of life from your spirit (and the Holy Spirit within) and the ultimate result will be sin. When you give in to temptation and sin, it originates from your flesh (soul + body), and not from your born-again spirit. The Lord wants you to draw from the Spirit within you, but instead, you yield to your flesh nature causing sin to become active or "alive" (Rom. 7:9). The apostle Paul makes it clear that our tussle is between the new nature in your born-again spirit and your fleshly desires.[7] It is not between your new nature and your old nature (the basis of two versions of yourself), as Jesus did not resurrect your old nature from the grave. Your old nature is dead and in the grave, so leave it alone. When you give in to your carnal desires and impulses, you no longer walk in the freedom for which Christ set you free (Gal. 5:1).

As a Christian walking in the flesh (as a carnal Christian), you begin to walk like a lost person with your understanding darkened, and you separate yourself from the flow of the life of God within you. Your thinking will become dominated by your passions and desires and not by the Spirit. This darkened understanding negatively affects you, your relationships, and your fellowship with God.

We all have a natural inclination to look in the wrong mirror, don't we, which results in wrong thinking and our adopting a wrong understanding of our identity. We return to thinking there are two versions of us and not just the new version of the new creation in Christ. When this occurs, we are dominated by what we can see, taste, hear, smell, and feel instead of God's Word. As a result, the flow of life from our born-again spirit stays turned off.

When you fail or sin (and we all occasionally do), you may think that God the Father is looking at your sin, but He is really looking at the new you, the 'real' you that is created in righteousness and holiness. Remember, the Father only sees one version of you, the new man (*anthropos*).

Why not develop a supernatural inclination to renew your mind and believe God's Word, so that your soul will agree with what has already transpired in your spirit?

---

[7] See the tussle between the Spirit and flesh in Galatians 5:16-17, 24-25; Romans 7:6-14, I Corinthians 3:1-3

When you sin, confess it right away! If you continue to sin, the love of God is not motivating your heart. Continuing to live in sin gives inroads for the devil to work in your life, violates unity and oneness with the Lord, and enslaves you once again. Thankfully, the Holy Spirit guides you to repent and not to repeat that sin in the future!

To summarize, your born-again spirit is *not* capable of sinning nor does sin originate from your spirit. As Jesus is NOW, so am I in this world – righteous, holy, perfect, and complete! This is not an excuse to sin, but should motivate you to stay pure in your Christian life!

Let's Discuss!

We learned that our born-again spirit is not capable of committing sin. How will you change your thinking so you see yourself as God the Father sees the 'real' you?

How Do You See Yourself?

Respond to this statement:

True or False: "I am a sinner saved by grace."

How you answer this statement tells a great deal about how you see yourself.

If you answer TRUE. . .

then as a Christian, you still see yourself as a *sinner*, having a *sin-consciousness* understanding of who you are. You still have an *inaccurate* understanding of your *I AM-ness*.

As a reminder, God only sees one version of you, the new man. He only has a righteousness view of you and doesn't see you as a sinner, but as a *saint*. He sees you as a *learner*, and not a loser or a failure. You need to see yourself the same way.

God sees you as a saint, not as a sinner. He sees you as a learner, and not a loser or a failure.

If you answer FALSE. . .

then you are seeing yourself with a *righteousness-consciousness,* and you are beginning to have an accurate understanding of your *I AM-ness*.

We might correct the statement this way (the way God sees you now!):

"I ~~am~~ *was* a sinner saved by grace; *now, I am a saint."*

You now stand on *righteousness-ground,* and no longer on condemnation-ground!

God sees the 'real you' (your born-again spirit) as *righteous, holy, perfect,* and *complete* as Jesus; therefore, you should as well.

The goal is to develop a *righteousness* consciousness where you no longer see yourself as a sinner (with a sin consciousness). Rather, you rightly see yourself as a righteous saint. (The term "saint" is a very frequent term for Christians in the New Testament.) You honestly and genuinely can say:

"I no longer see myself as a sinner, but as a saint. . . who occasionally sins."

God does not see you as a 'sin' consciousness person; He sees you as having a 'righteous' nature, since that is how He has recreated you! That's the gold standard.

> "I am a saint who occasionally sins" needs to be your mindset.

Let's Internalize and Apply!

1. As a Christian, you are a born-again spirit, you have a soul, and you live in a body. So what is the 'real you'?

   ____

   ____

2. When God the Father looks at you, what does He see?

   ____

   ____

3. What is the difference between having a *sin-consciousness* and a *righteousness consciousness*? How can you move to having a righteousness consciousness, the gold standard?

____

____

4. When you sin (and we all do occasionally), does your born-again spirit participate?

____

____

5. True/False: The Father has a righteousness view of you and only sees you as a *saint,* and never a sinner.

6. True/False: The members of the Godhead see you as a *learner*, and not a loser or a failure.

Section 2

The Role of Repentance

"not laying again a foundation of repentance from dead works. . ." Hebrews 6:1

"how much more will the blood of Christ. . .cleanse your conscience from dead works to serve the living God? Hebrews 9:14

Hebrews chapter 6:1-3 records that there are six principles of Christ that are foundation stones upon which our Christian faith is built that are necessary to proceed to maturity. They are:

- Repentance from Dead Works
- Faith in God
- Doctrine of Baptisms
- Laying on of Hands
- Resurrection of the Dead
- Eternal Judgment

We will learn about the first two principles: *Repentance from dead works* and *faith in God* in this book. Implementing these two principles activates what Christ did for you to make possible how Father God sees and knows you. As you will learn, there is first a *putting off* (repentance from dead works) followed by a *putting on* (faith in God).[8] In this section, you will learn the putting-off phase: repentance from dead works. In the next section, Section 3, you will learn about the putting-on phase – faith in God.

Father God wants you to have a clear conscience before Him and others. To live with a good conscience requires repentance from dead works coupled with faith in God. A good conscience is a two-step process.

Repentance from our dead works – our efforts to please God – is required to receive His forgiveness of our sins so that we experience a clear conscience. Repentance from dead works is fully experienced when you feel the love of the Father without any sense of condemnation from God, from the devil, or from yourself.

[8] We will only learn about the first two principles of Christ in this book. To learn about all six principles, please get our book, *Foundation Stones: 6 Principles to Maturity in Christ.*

In Chapter 6, *Winning in the Courtroom of Heaven*, you will learn about the spiritual context where repentance occurs.

In Chapter 7, *Repentance from Dead Works,* you will learn about the term *repentance* and then about what *dead works* means.

In Chapter 8, *The Completeness of Forgiveness*, you will learn about the completeness of the Father's forgiveness for you. Not understanding the completeness of forgiveness, you will not feel really forgiven. You will return and repent of those same things again and again.

In Chapter 9, *The Gift of a Good Conscience*, you will learn how to maintain a clear conscience and fully accept your identity in Christ.

Finally, in Chapter 10, "*Give Me Back My Stuff*," you will learn how to return to a good conscience when such things as negativity, shame, guilt, and anxiety get in the way of a good conscience before God.

Chapter 6

Winning in the Courtroom of Heaven

To understand the first two principles – *repentance from dead works* and *faith in God* – in a more complete way, it is helpful to know how they function or operate in the spirit realm. The Bible places prayer in general, and repentance and confession in particular, in a courtroom or judicial setting in the spirit realm. In Heaven, there are many different courts that operate (Zech. 3:7). We are not told how many courts there are or their purpose, but it seems plausible that there are different courtrooms set up for different spheres or jurisdictions on the earth.

We do know that the courts of Heaven are *legal places* in the spirit realm in which we can operate. Perhaps you may not have thought of repentance, confession, and forgiveness as something that occurs in the courtroom of Heaven, but it is the case. Repentance that results in forgiveness is a legal transaction that happens in a courtroom in the spirit realm. We gain victory first in the spiritual realm and that affects the physical realm.

Who and what speaks for you in the Courts of Heaven? We have great news for you! Hebrews 12:24 records that the shed blood of Christ *"speaks better things"* about you before the Judge of all. The blood of Jesus answers every accusation against you. Jesus, who is at the right hand of God, always lives to make intercession for you.[9] He speaks for you as your advocate and defense attorney.

First the Courtroom, then the Battlefield

In Scripture, the place of the initial victory is in a courtroom and not on a battlefield. The first place of prayer and repentance should be in the courtroom of Heaven. It is there that we must first win our verdicts before going out to win on the battlefield.

> Jesus never pictures prayer in a battlefield context; He placed prayer in a courtroom or judicial setting.

The first thing we must do to step into the courts of Heaven is to get off of the battlefield. We must gain legal victory through repentance before we run to the battle. We are in a conflict

[9] See Romans 8:34; Hebrews 7:25

with our adversary, but it is a legal one. Jesus never pictures prayer in a battlefield context; He placed prayer in a courtroom or judicial setting. The verdict from the court is the legal "wrestling," and putting the Judge's "not guilty" verdict into place is the battlefield part. The proceedings in the courtroom always come before the victory on the battlefield.

The problem is that many Christians believe that when they pray they are on a battlefield. They rush into a conflict without securing a verdict from Heaven. This is a critical mistake that has caused us to experience defeat, chaos, and backlash from our adversary. We rush into places of prayer only to see things get worse rather than better. This is because we stir things up on the battlefield without first having established a legal precedent to be there. We must first get off the battlefield and into the courtroom.

> The proceedings in the courtroom always come before the victory on the battlefield.

Let's Apply!

Has it been your practice to go onto the battlefield to secure a victory before first going to the courts of Heaven? If so, what will you do to reverse this practice?

Once an issue is settled in Heaven, things will change in your life. It takes some legal wrangling to set this in place but once it is done, we can march onto the battlefield and win every time. Go to the third heaven and get favorable verdicts in the courts of Heaven before going to the battlefield in the second heaven. We have the best lawyer and Advocate – Jesus! And better yet, His Father is the Judge. The odds are in your favor with this Judge and your Lawyer, as long as you follow the proper protocol: repent and apply the cleansing blood of Christ to your life first.

We pray the prayer of repentance in the courts of Heaven, as it were, to eliminate the adversary's right to function in our life. Your adversary can only hinder you because he has a legal right to do so.

For context, there are three heavens referred to in scripture. The *first* heaven is the physical heaven, what our physical eyes see. The *second* heaven is the realm where spiritual activity takes place, the work of both angels and demons. It is the realm of principalities and powers and is where spiritual warfare takes place.[10]

---

[10] See Ephesians 6:12; 2 Corinthians 10:4-5

The *third* heaven is the spiritual layer above the other two heavens. This is the highest realm in both location and authority. It is the residence of God, the place where His throne is located, as well as the Courts of Heaven. It is the place where Jesus ascended after His resurrection and the eternal home of the saints. Our third heaven authority originates from the position of being seated above all, with Christ in heaven. You are a third-heaven creation operating in third-heaven revelation with the capacity of functioning in third-heaven authority.[11]

The Courts of Heaven

The prophet Daniel saw a glimpse of the Courts of the third heaven in operation. Daniel 7:9-10 unveils the judicial system of heaven.

> *I kept looking*
> *Until thrones were set up,*
> *And the Ancient of Days took His seat;*
> *His vesture was like white snow*
> *And the hair of His head like pure wool.*
> *His throne was ablaze with flames,*
> *Its wheels were a burning fire.*
> *A river of fire was flowing*
> *And coming out from before Him;*
> *Thousands upon thousands were attending Him,*
> *And myriads upon myriads were standing before Him;*
> *The court sat,*
> *And the books were opened.*

Daniel beheld the Father as the Ancient of Days ruling over the courts of Heaven. He is the One who renders decisions from this Court that alter life on Earth. When this Court sets a decision in place, there is no appealing or altering it.

Later in Daniel 7:22, 26-27, we see verdicts of the court of Heaven against the kingdom of darkness.

[11] See 2 Corinthians 12:2; Ephesians 2:6; Colossians 1:16

> *Until the Ancient of Days came and judgment was passed in favor of the saints of the Highest One, and the time arrived when the saints took possession of the kingdom.*
>
> *But the court will sit for judgment, and his* [the devil's] *dominion will be taken away, annihilated and destroyed forever.*
>
> *Then the sovereignty, the dominion and the greatness of all the kingdoms under the whole heaven will be given to the people of the saints of the Highest One; His kingdom will be an everlasting kingdom, and all the dominions will serve and obey Him.*

In this passage, the arrogance and rebellion of the devil and his workers are judged and destroyed by courtroom verdicts of the Judge of all. Applying this protocol to you and me, when we repent in the context of the court of Heaven, we are set free from demonic interference that previously affected us. Notice that one verdict from this Court moves the saints (you and me) from defeat to dominion. This all occurred because of a single verdict or decision from this Court.

It's in the courts of Heaven that you will see victory claimed for you and your family. This Court is the place where you make your case that allows divine decisions to be rendered by the Father, the Righteous Judge on your behalf. This is the place where you operate in authority.

Other passages which show a heavenly courtroom in session include: The court with other divine beings participating in the discussion with God as described by the prophet Micaiah to kings Jehoshaphat and Ahab (I Kings 22: 19-23), and the court of Heaven in operation as the sons of God and Satan were brought before the court regarding Job (Job 1:6-12; 2:1-6).

Jesus actually placed prayer in a judicial setting, and not on a battlefield.

Prayer is Placed in a Judicial Setting

One of the reasons we know we have influence in the Courts is because Jesus actually placed prayer in a judicial setting, and not on a battlefield. In Luke 18, Jesus told a story or parable of a widow coming before an unjust judge. An adversary had a legal case against her. Through her persistent presentation of her case, the judge gave her a right verdict.

> *Now He was telling them a parable to show that at all times they ought to pray and not to lose heart, saying, "In a certain city there was a judge who did not fear God and did not respect man. There was a widow in that city, and she kept coming to him, saying, 'Give me legal protection from my opponent.' For a while he was unwilling; but afterward he said to himself, 'Even though I do not fear God nor respect man, yet because this widow bothers me, I will give her legal protection, otherwise by continually coming she will wear me out.' " And the Lord said, "Hear what the unrighteous judge said; now, will not God bring about justice for His elect who cry to Him day and night, and will He delay long over them? I tell you that He will bring about justice for them quickly. However, when the Son of Man comes, will He find faith on the earth?"* (Luke 18:1-8)

The whole moral to the story is that if this widow, without any influence or power, could convince a judge to render a verdict in her favor, how much more can we come before God the righteous Judge and see Him favor us in His decisions. There are several things we learn about approaching God as Judge.

First, the Father is the Judge and rules over the judicial system of heaven and will render decisions for us from His Courts. He is an *impartial* Judge of *all* that is done on the earth.[12]

Second, we are invited to come and present our cases in the courts of Heaven. Hebrews 4:16 directs us to boldly come *"to the throne of grace, so that we may receive mercy and find grace to help in time of need."* After all, we are already seated in heavenly places at the right hand of the Father because we are in Christ Jesus (Eph. 2:6). Do you see yourself seated there? And in Isaiah 43:26, the Father, using courtroom language, directs us to present our case:

> *Put Me in remembrance, let us argue our case together;*
> *State your cause, that you may be proved right* [acquitted].

Putting God in remembrance as a means of presenting cases in His Courts is essential. Our Judge can only render decisions based on evidence presented. We must know how to present cases in the Courts of Heaven to get favorable verdicts.

---

[12] See Hebrews 12:23; I Pet. 1:17

In the story of the widow in Luke 18, when she wanted justice:

- The widow went to the courtroom and not the battlefield. The widow realized she didn't need to march onto a battlefield and yell at her adversary. She simply needed a verdict from the court.

- She didn't even address her adversary; she only spoke to the judge. She understood that if the Judge rendered a legal verdict, any power of the adversary would be demolished and she would win. Once this was in place her adversary had to bow the knee to the rendering of the court.

In our case, there is no need to yell, scream, or even curse our foe. All we need is a legal decision based on a verdict from Heaven and the fight is over. We can then make decrees after we revoke the enemy's legal claim in the court of Heaven.

The courts of Heaven are the place where our case against the devil is heard. In this place, the devil's claim is revoked. The courts of Heaven is for the elect and chosen of God. We don't have to fear this place but enter the Courts with great confidence by the blood of Jesus (Heb. 10:19). Romans 8:33 tells us that as the elect of God, no charge against us can stick.

> *Who will bring a charge* [in the courts of Heaven] *against God's <u>elect</u>? God is the one who justifies. (bracket and underline added)*

You are the elect or chosen of God based on Jesus' blood, the Holy Spirit's work, and God's heart toward you (1 Peter 1:1-2). You and I have status as the elect of God before His Courts. As Jesus speaks of the widow that keeps presenting her case, He declares that this is what the *elect* of God should do. The courts of Heaven are the place where we take our adversary to Court to be judged and to get a favorable verdict.

Returning to the story in Luke 18, there are several things to notice that will help us in presenting cases in the Courts of Heaven. Notice that the woman has an *adversary.* In Luke 18:3 NKJV, she was asking for judgment and justice from her adversary.

> *Now there was a widow in that city; and she came to him, saying, "Get justice for me from my <u>adversary</u>."*

The Greek word for *adversary* is *antidikos* which means "an opponent in a lawsuit." In your life and your family, you have a legal opponent that is resisting the will of God. First Peter 5:8 clearly lets us know that this *adversary* is looking for legal means to devour and destroy.

> *Be of sober spirit, be on the alert. Your adversary, the devil, prowls around like a roaring lion, seeking someone to devour.*

This word adversary in this verse is the same in the Greek that we found in Luke 18:3. It declares that we have a *legal opponent.* We are to be on guard against this legal agent, who is the devil. Otherwise, he will claim the legal right to devour and destroy the will, the desire, and intent of God in your life.

We as the elect of God have the right to counter-sue and bring a case against our adversary.

Jesus' key take-away was this: If this widow could get a decision rendered, how much more can we as the *elect of God*. This means that the courtroom of Heaven is the place where the *elect* bring cases against our adversary. Remember that the *adversary* is the one who is attacking us with a lawsuit. However, we as the elect of God have the right to counter-sue and bring a case against our adversary. In the context of *repentance from dead works*, we repent of our efforts to earn God's acceptance and apply the blood of Christ to them before the Judge of all. Father God, the impartial Judge of all, then renders a favorable verdict for you as the elect of God! This is the *best way* to do spiritual warfare.

Jesus' Manner of Spiritual Warfare

Because you have a legal opponent or adversary, you should follow Jesus' manner of warfare against the devil. Revelation 19:11 gives us great insight into how Jesus Himself deals with His adversaries.

> *And I saw heaven opened, and behold, a white horse, and He who sat on it is called Faithful and True, and in righteousness He judges and wages war.*

Notice that Jesus has an order in which He does warfare: He *judges*, then *makes war*.

- *Judging* is judicial activity in a courtroom (i.e., for us, getting favorable verdicts based upon evidence – repent and apply the blood of Christ) and

- *waging war* is battlefield activity (i.e., for us, binding and loosing, declarations, decrees).

Jesus has an order in which He does warfare: He *judges*, then *makes war*.

To try to make war without a favorable verdict or judgment from the court of Heaven is to suffer defeat because you have no legal footing to be on the battlefield. Anytime you challenge your adversary who claims a legal right, he will withstand you. Backlash occurs when sin-based legal claims have not been addressed in the Courts through repentance and renouncing your words and actions, which open the door for the enemy. Until the legal claims of the enemy are addressed, don't be surprised that an agitated spirit realm stirs up a reaction in the natural realm.

Once you get the legal rendering from the Father, our righteous Judge, then you can march onto the battlefield and win every time. The problem has been that we have tried to win on the battlefield without legal verdicts from Heaven backing us up. So, go into the courts of Heaven, repent and apply the blood of Jesus to cancel these sin-based legal claims against you to remove their influence and power.

Go into the Courts of Heaven, take the blood of Jesus, and cancel these sin-based legal claims against you.

This means to first go into what the apostle Paul called the third heaven to the courts of Heaven to remove the claims against you or your family, and then go to the second heaven (where spiritual warfare is waged) and remove the enemy's influence and power (2 Cor. 12:2) using your authority to bind his efforts. To summarize, begin in the third heaven to revoke the claim and then move to the second heaven to remove the enemy. Then the Spirit of God can flow freely in your life.

We hope you have gained a better understanding of how powerful repentance is in the courts of Heaven. Make it a practice to enter the courts of Heaven to remove the legal claims of the devil and walk in the freedom Christ has provided to you.

Let's Internalize and Apply!

1. True/False: In Scripture, the place of initial victory is the courtroom and not a battlefield.

   ____

   ____

2. Where are the Courts of Heaven located?

   ____

   ____

3. True/False: You are a third-heaven creation operating in third-heaven revelation with the capacity of functioning in third-heaven authority.

4. True/False: You don't need to address your adversary in the Court of Heaven, but only speak (repent) to the Judge of all.

5. True/False: You are the elect or chosen of God based on Jesus' blood, the Holy Spirit's work, and God's heart toward you.

6. What is Jesus' order in which He does warfare?

   ____

   ____

Chapter 7

Repenting from Dead Works

In our journey to maturity, the first foundation stone we must put in place is repentance from dead works – turning away from our human efforts to please God.

The Lord wants you to have a clear conscience in His presence. He wants you to feel totally loved and accepted by Papa God with nothing standing between the two of you. However, we are often programmed by religion and at times by culture to think that we can earn the Father's love and acceptance through our human efforts, our good works, or our religious traditions. The scripture calls these efforts, *dead works.*

Dead works are efforts or works that are lifeless, that have no life in them (Gal. 3:21). They cannot justify or make us accepted before God. The scripture is very clear that none of our human efforts or traditions result in God's forgiveness and acceptance: *"There is no one who does good, not even one"* (Ps. 53:3).

Regarding those who rely on their religious tradition (such as keeping the 10 Commandments or the Law), the scripture states: *"by the works of the Law no flesh is justified in His sight* (Rom. 3:20). The purpose of the Law was never to make us acceptable to God but *"to shut up everyone under sin"* (Gal. 3:22). Holding on to our human efforts to keep the Law leaves us with a *sin-consciousness* which we learned about in a previous chapter.

The Law leads *"us to Christ, so that we may be justified by faith"* (Gal. 3:24). For *"by grace you have been saved through faith; and that not of yourselves, it is the gift of God"* (Eph. 2:8). The apostle Paul described God's grace wonderfully in Titus 3:5-7:

> *He saved us, not on the basis of deeds which we have done in righteousness, but according to His mercy, by the washing of regeneration and renewing by the Holy Spirit, whom He poured out upon us richly through Jesus Christ our Savior, so that being justified by His grace we would be made heirs according to the hope of eternal life.*

Dead works are associated with your old nature that was crucified with Jesus at the cross and left in the grave. As a Christian, the Godhead only sees one version of you – the new man in Christ. Your old nature – including your dead works, human efforts, and traditions – were nailed to the cross and do not speak on your behalf before the Father. When you adopt God's *new man* version of you, you understand that your nature and identity is righteousness --and is the basis of having a *righteousness-consciousness* view of yourself.

Dead works are associated with your old nature that was crucified at the Cross and left in the grave.

Unless we turn from dead works, our worship of God is in vain. God wants us to be totally dependent upon Him. When we emphasize our works, we are trying to make ourselves more acceptable and presentable to God. The only thing that makes us worthy to come into His presence is the blood of Jesus Christ.

> *Knowing that you were not redeemed with perishable things. . . but with precious blood, as of a lamb unblemished and spotless, the blood of Christ.* (I Peter 1:18-19)

Repentance is the process our loving heavenly Father has provided for you to clear the slate of dead works and obtain a clean conscience with the Father. Where does repentance occur? As we learned in the previous chapter, repentance occurs in the courts of Heaven in the unseen realm of the spirit.

Repentance in the Courtroom

Hebrews 12:24 records that the shed blood of Christ *"speaks better things"* about you before the Judge of all. Jesus brought His own blood into the holy place in heaven to speak on your behalf (Heb. 9:12). The blood of Jesus answers every accusation against you and your bloodline. Jesus' blood cries for mercy, redemption, and forgiveness for you. As a result of the testimony of the blood of Jesus on your behalf, God now has the legal right He needed to forgive you. His heart has always desired to forgive but He needed the legal right to do so. You simply need to repent of your sins (of dead works) and agree with the testimony of Jesus' blood, and receive His forgiveness because of what the blood is speaking.

It's by faith that you apply the blood of the Lord Jesus Christ. In that the blood speaks, it is declaring and gives judicial testimony on your behalf. Jesus' blood silences every voice that would dare to speak against you. It's in the heavenly courtroom where you remind the Judge of the finished work of Christ on your behalf. The death, burial, resurrection, and ascension of Christ was the legal transaction that enables the Father to forgive you of your sins.

When we know how to present this evidence in the courts of Heaven, we get the full benefit of all Jesus has done for us. We can say, "Let it be known or recorded in the courts of Heaven that the blood of Christ speaks of better things about me" (Mal. 3:16).

Here is a model prayer to help you understand and reinforce the context of repentance in the courts of Heaven in the spiritual realm:

> Lord, I come to stand before Your Courts and I want to remind You that Jesus' blood is speaking on my behalf. I thank You for the forgiveness that is mine as a result of what His blood says about me. I repent of any and every sin of dead works and ask for Jesus' blood to speak and testify for me. Thank you, Father, that Your heart is always looking to forgive. The blood of Jesus grants You the legal right You needed. I ask for the blood of Jesus to speak for me before Your Courts. I agree with what the blood is saying about me. I ask the Court to render a decision based on the testimony of His blood on my behalf. I ask, therefore, that every accusation against me because of my sins would now be forgiven and removed. Thank You Father so much for Your forgiveness and redemption. Amen.

Your part is to repent – confess as sin --the wrong thinking about acceptance in the eyes of your Father. God's part then is to forgive you. As a result, you gain a clear conscience before God. The Father deeply desires for you to have a good conscience before Him and live dependent upon Him. The Christian life, by design, is meant to be a life of dependency. You are never going to please God by living independent from Him. Genuine repentance brings in the presence of God.

Repentance means "to change one's mind." Repentance is a sincere turning away from wrong thinking. Changing your mind away from wrong thinking is the first step. The second step is to live with a new way of thinking that aligns with God's ways, will, and Word. For repentance to have its full work, there must be a *turning from* your dead works and a *turning to* Christ.

Agreeing with Our Adversary

Humility and surrender carry great weight in the courts of Heaven. Through repentance you set in place the voice of the blood of Jesus. When you sense your adversary bringing accusations against you, you should simply agree with them. This is so opposite of what your mind tells you to do. Why? Because you want to justify yourself. But Jesus says we are to agree with our adversary quickly.

> *Agree with your adversary quickly, while you are on the way with him, let your adversary deliver you to the judge, the judge hand you over to the officer, and you be thrown into prison. (Matthew 5:25 NKJV).*

To quickly agree with your adversary simply means that you are quick to repent of anything being used against you in the Courts. Lon speaking: My approach is I have no need to justify myself; I allow the blood of Jesus to justify and speak for me. My attitude is that I can never go wrong with repentance. Self-justification can destroy me, but repentance will cause me to be accepted. As I repent of anything in my history or even bloodline issues, the Lord will grant me repentance (2 Tim. 2:25). This takes away the accusations of the devil and silences his ability to disqualify me. If I want to have an audience in the courts, I must appear there with a humble spirit and a contrite heart (Ps. 51:17).

The End-Goal: A Clear Conscience

Repentance leads to forgiveness that results in a clear conscience, the goal the Lord has had all along. There are two types of wrong thinking that hinder us from living with a clear conscience. You have just been introduced to the first way: *having a conscience distorted by dead works*. (We will learn of the second hinderance, *having an evil conscience*, in an upcoming chapter).

Dead works is the erroneous notion that God accepts you based on your performance (*My Doing*), rather than what Jesus has done with your sins (*His Doing*).[13] Hebrews 9:14 tells us:

---

[13] You may want to review Chapter 3 His Doing vs My Doing if you want to refresh your understanding of this truth.

> *. . .how much more will the blood of Christ . . . cleanse your conscience from dead works to serve the living God*? (Hebrews 9:14, underline added)

When you received Christ as your Savior, your spirit was cleansed of its sin nature, but you may not have purged your conscience with the truth about what Jesus has done with your sins. Satan will drag up things you have done or said to convince you that God no longer accepts you and you must *do* something to be accepted once again. Don't allow your own negative self-talk or the devil's condemnation to destroy your faith and confidence in God's acceptance. This wrong thinking will lead you to believe you don't deserve His forgiveness and favor.

Reject the lie that your acceptance by God is based on what you do and *embrace* the truth that He accepts you based 100% on Jesus' finished work. Repent and apply the cleansing blood of Christ to all of your sins and works in order to gain and live in the Father's acceptance.

Let's Discuss!

When you sin, do you ever feel condemned? How should you respond?

What does it mean to have a "righteousness-consciousness?"

Let's Internalize and Apply!

1. What are dead works?

    ____

    ____

2. How do you cleanse your conscience of "dead works?"

    ____

    ____

Chapter 8

The Completeness of Forgiveness

One of the most important understandings about your born-again spirit is:

> "I am completely forgiven of all my sins – past, present, and future."

From our experience in ministry, this truth is one of the most difficult for many Christians to understand and accept as true. You, too, may find it hard to believe and accept that the "war" between you and God regarding your sins is over and God is not mad at you. We have found that once believers understand, believe, and accept this pivotal truth of complete forgiveness, so many other truths are much easier to believe and activate. Therefore, this chapter is devoted to the subject of your complete forgiveness.

So let's look into God's spiritual mirror of the Scriptures at six aspects about your complete forgiveness. This chapter is a somewhat heavy chapter to read, but it is essential that you understand complete forgiveness in order to move forward.

First, God has forever settled the sin issue. God is not crediting or applying sin against anyone. God has not credited sin to anyone for nearly 2,000 years. The sins of the entire world have been paid for but you only benefit from this if you repent when you do sin.

I John 2:1-2 states:

> *. . . and if anyone sins, we have an Advocate with the Father, Jesus Christ the righteous; and He Himself is the propitiation for our sins; and not for ours only, but also for those of the whole world.*

Not only are your sins as a Christian forgiven and paid for, the sins of the lost have been paid for as well. Jesus bore the sins of everyone – not just those He knew would accept Him. People aren't really going to hell because of sin. They're going to hell because they have rejected Jesus' payment for their sins.

If you think God is angry with you and is holding your sins against you, then you'll never have boldness, confidence, or faith. The truth of the matter is God is not angry with you about anything once you are born again.

Jesus—who knew no sin, did no sin, and in Him was no sin -- bore the condemnation of every sin ever committed. When Jesus ascended from the grave to sit at the right hand of the Father, there was no sin upon Him because He paid the penalty for all sin at the Cross. There is no sin upon us, either, because we are in Him. Your sins were left in the grave, because they did not make it through the resurrection.

You don't want to sin. But when you do, you are not condemned (I John 2:1 above) since your sins have already been judged and condemned at the Cross. When you sin, the Holy Spirit will convict you (not condemn you) to draw you back into unity with the Lord. Let us not grieve the Holy Spirit by failing to repent of a sin.

God does not hold a sin against you that Jesus has already paid for.

God does not hold a sin against you that Jesus has already paid for. If He did, God would be putting us in double jeopardy for a sin that Jesus already paid for.

Second, you are forgiven of all sin – past, present, and future. God has forgiven you of all your sin, even sins you have not committed yet. God is no longer angry because you sin! Your forgiveness has been provided for and you *apply* that forgiveness when you confess a sin or failure.

> *. . .but through His own blood, He entered the holy place once for all, having obtained eternal redemption. . . those who have been called may receive the promise of the eternal inheritance.* (Hebrews 9:12c, 15, underline added)

> *. . .we have been sanctified* [positionally] *through the offering of the body of Jesus Christ once for all. . . For by one offering He has perfected for all time those who are sanctified* [process]. (Hebrews 10:10, 14, brackets added)

> *. . . and to the spirits of the righteous made perfect.* (Hebrews 12:23)

These verses show that you are forgiven of all past, present, and future sins *as you appropriate* this truth. God remembers *covenant*. The devil remembers *sin*. You get to choose which one you agree with.

Let's Discuss!

What makes it difficult for you to see yourself as your Heavenly Father sees you – as righteous, holy, perfect and complete as you will ever be? Explain.

Do you find it hard to accept the truth that the sins you have committed are already forgiven?

When Jesus died on the cross for your sins, how many of them were in the future at that time?

Third, since you are born again, sin will never be an issue between you and God.

Question: Does this mean that you can just go live in sin?

Absolutely not! How shall you being dead in your relationship to sin return to revive the power of sin in your life? This would be returning to bondage. As a new creation, you have been set free of the power of sin! You do not want to go back and live in sin. Why?

Sin enslaves.

> *. . .when you present yourselves to someone as slaves for obedience, you are slaves of the one whom you obey, either of sin resulting in death, or of obedience resulting in righteousness?* Romans 6:16
>
> *Stand fast therefore in the liberty by which Christ has made us free, and do not be entangled again with a yoke of bondage.* Galatians 5:1 NKJV

Even though you are in Christ, the flesh remains dormant within you. In your born-again spirit, you are dead in your relationship to sin, so do not return to sin and revive it again! If you revive the flesh, you resurrect it and it is no longer dormant. The "beast" in you is sleeping, it's not dead. Choose to not walk according to the flesh (our old nature) but walk according to the Spirit (in our born-again spirit).

> *Even so consider yourselves to be dead to sin, but alive to God in Christ Jesus. (*Romans 6:11)

In your spirit, you are dead in your relationship to sin, so do not return to sin and revive it again!

Consider yourself dead to sin. The Father does.

You do not have to sin. To do so is to allow sin to "reign" in your mortal body. If you do, you certainly will not lose your salvation, but you will suffer the consequences of choosing to live *independent* of God. Do not get entangled again with a yoke (or attachment) to sin. If you sin, "crucify the flesh with its passions and desires" (Gal. 5:24). Put it to death by repenting and applying the blood of Christ to it! Your born-again spirit desires purity and liberty, that which is holy and righteous, so follow your spirit.

> *Having these promises, beloved, let us cleanse ourselves from all defilement of flesh and spirit, perfecting holiness in the fear of God. (*2 Corinthians 7:1)

Sinning violates the unity you have with the Lord and your spiritual oneness with Him.

You have the responsibility to safeguard your body from sin and keep it from being used as an instrument of unrighteousness. Failing to do so would be to *violate the unity* you have with the Lord and your spiritual oneness with Him. Sinning against your own body involves sinning against the Jesus to whom you are united, allowing sin to reign in your mortal body.

> *. . .consider yourselves to be dead to sin, but alive to God in Christ Jesus. Therefore do not let sin reign in your mortal body so that you obey its lusts.* **(**Romans 6:11-12)

In Christ, your relationship to sin has died. But when you give in to the temptation to sin as a Christian, you are once again giving sin power in your life by resurrecting it. The power of the flesh (soul + body) is strong and alluring, but when it makes its appeal, you don't have to respond. Choose to firmly resist temptation and preserve the unity you have with Jesus!

Sin gives an inroad for Satan to work in your life.

If you go out and live in sin, you're inviting Satan in. You're opening a door for the devil to work in your life.

Sinning is foolish. If you choose to live in sin, you're not smart. But God loves you. God is not holding your sin against you, but you are inviting the devil into your life. You are not going to prosper if you choose to live in sin. You will hinder, handicap, and even nullify the grace of God because you are not cooperating with God. You are called to freedom, so stay free!

> *For you were called to freedom, brethren; only do not turn your freedom into an opportunity for the flesh, but through love serve one another.* **(**Galatians 5:13)

Sin, whether in word or action, results in a bad harvest.

There is an overriding principle in scripture that every seed sown will result in a harvest. While the earth remains, there will always be seedtime and harvest. With our words, we either speak words of life or words of death. Words and actions of life and death have been set before us, resulting in a harvest of blessing or of death. We are commanded to choose life with our words and our actions. Jesus tells us that seedtime and harvest is how the kingdom of God works. There will always be a harvest. (Gen. 8:22; Prov. 18:21; Deut. 30:19; Mark 4:26-29).

Take a few minutes now and ask Holy Spirit to examine your heart to identity any negative seeds you have sown with your words or your actions. You only want a good harvest and not a bad one. Pray this prayer to cancel negative words and actions:

> "Lord, forgive me for every harmful word I have spoken against myself or others, and in the mighty name of Jesus Christ, I take authority over and cancel and break the power of every harmful or negative word I have spoken about me or others. Any assignment the enemy has put in motion by such words, let it be cancelled and nullified now in Jesus' name.
>
> In the mighty name of Jesus Christ, I break off any assignment, plot, and scheme by the enemy that my words have opened doors to and cancel their effect over my life, my family, even the nation. I command any doors opened through such action be legally closed now in the name of Jesus Christ. Let no word curse, or negative words spoken by me take root in my life and bear harmful fruit. Let it be uprooted now in Jesus' name.
>
> I speak life and life more abundant and blessing over my life, my family's life, over others, and the nation in Jesus' name. In the name of Jesus Christ, Lord, order my words, let them be released in authority, in power, in wisdom, and be pleasing and acceptable to You, in Jesus' name."

Fourth, God does not impute (hold) sin against you and will not hold future sin against you.

> . . .*just as David also speaks of the blessing on the man to whom God credits* [imputes] *righteousness apart from works: Blessed are those whose lawless deeds have been forgiven* [past tense]*, and whose sins have been covered* [past tense]; *Blessed is the man whose sin the Lord will not* [future tense] *take into account* [impute sin]." (Romans 4:6-8, brackets added)

Your actions or wrong thinking do not define your identity in Christ.

This verse says God "will not" impute (credit) *sin* to you, because He has already imputed *righteousness* to you. Everything is a legal matter in the courts of Heaven when it comes to Heaven and the spirit realm. When you were born again, all of your sins – past, present, and even future sins – were laid on Jesus. God will never in the future hold sins against you! When you do sin, it is your responsibility to confess that sin and thank God that this sin has already been forgiven. In so doing, you are not letting sin negatively affect your heart, your body, and your relationships.

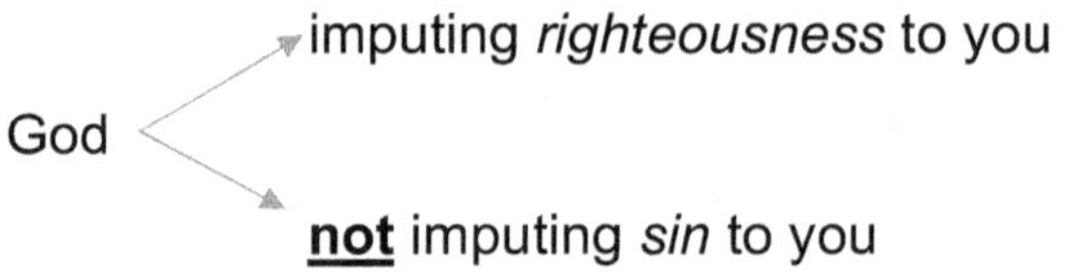

Christ's finished work is not benefiting you if you fall into religious thinking that says,

> "I've been saved by grace, but now that I am a Christian, I need to pray, fast, tithe, study, and attend church in order for God to love me, bless me, use me, and answer my prayers."

You know that God is powerful, but you may think, "How could He ever use His power on my behalf?" This puts you back under a sin-consciousness rather than a righteous-consciousness, thinking you have to perform to keep God's favor. You begin to doubt God's willingness to use His ability on your behalf because you feel He is still holding sin against you.

This is religion speaking and not the Bible. Religion puts the focus on what *you* need to do instead of what *Christ* has already done. Religion is all about your "doing" – that's behavior modification.

Your acceptance is found at the Cross because the Father was fully satisfied with Jesus' payment for your sins. Now, your heavenly Father assesses you based on what Jesus has already done. When you do sin, repent and thank Him that this sin is forgiven. Remember, to the extent that God the Father is *satisfied* with Jesus' finished work, He is *satisfied with you*!

In summary, God placed all your sin upon Jesus. All your sin. Sin is a non-issue with God. He is aware of when you sin and will strongly impress upon you to quit doing it, but not because He's going to reject you. He's already paid for it. God is not ignorant of sin in your life, but it does not change His attitude toward you. Holy Spirit will point to that sin in your life as a place of your next upgrade in your relationship with the Father. Jesus paid for your sin – past, present, and even future sins. When God looks at you, He sees your born-again spirit – which is as eternally righteous and holy as Jesus!

What you may have done (sin, failure) is *not* who you are. Your actions or wrong thinking do not define your identity in Christ. What God has said about you, and provided through Jesus Christ, defines your identity.

Let's Discuss!

Do you feel that God is imputing or holding a sin against you? If so, are you thinking with a 'sin consciousness' or with a 'righteousness consciousness?'

How can you flip the script to see God imputing righteousness to you?

Fifth, God does not put a timeline on your forgiveness!

Every time you sin, the Lord doesn't have to wait until you repent in order to get that sin under the Blood and then be forgiven. Our redemption in Christ was not a short-term redemption – that is, only good until the next time you sin (and then have to repent, get the Blood reapplied, and be forgiven again).

The truth is Christ entered the holy place once and obtained for us an *eternal* redemption. God's grace is *cheapened* when you think He has only forgiven you of your sins up to the point you are saved, and after that point, you must depend on your confession of sins to be forgiven. God's forgiveness is not given in *installments*.

If you believe God's forgiveness is given in installments, you won't be able to expect God to protect, provide, and prosper you. It will rob you of your ability to receive God's goodness, blessings, unmerited favor, and success.

God's forgiveness is not given in *installments*.

Lon speaking: *This truth about no timeline on forgiveness was very difficult for me to accept for a number of years. I felt that my sins were forgiven up to a point – up to the most recent time that I confessed my sins – but not since that time. I felt He was still holding these latter sins against me. This is what religion had taught me, and not the Bible. Religion had put the focus on what I needed to do instead of what Christ has already done.*

I was living with a sin consciousness with a pretty strong emotional attachment to that wrong understanding. I was listening to the wrong voice (religion) rather than God's voice that says I am completely forgiven of all my sins – past, present, and future. Now, I have the Spirit's revelation of the completeness of God's forgiveness. I am free to live with a righteousness consciousness in my born-again spirit; I am completely forgiven!

So now when I sin, I quickly repent of it out of my love for the Lord and thank Him that this sin was forgiven on the Cross two-thousand years ago. I rejoice that my loving heavenly Father forgave me of all my sins and I appropriate that forgiveness when I repent!

Let's Discuss!

Do you put a timeline on God's forgiveness of your sins?

Do you feel that God has only forgiven you up to a point in time?

Moving forward, how can you regularly appropriate God's forgiveness on an on-going basis?

Sixth, God has completely qualified you in your standing before Him! He has qualified you for all His blessings through the shed blood of Jesus Christ on the cross, and His burial and resurrection.

> *giving thanks to the Father, who has qualified us to share in the inheritance of the saints in Light.* (Colossians 1:12, underline added)

Do you ever feel unqualified for God's acceptance? We have good news! You are fully qualified to share in the full inheritance that is yours!

Don't fall into the trap of looking at your life, imperfections and failings, and start to disqualify yourself from receiving God's blessings and favor. You may be tempted to think, "Why would God bless me? Look at what I've done. I am so undeserving." Instead of having faith to believe God for breakthroughs, you may feel too condemned to believe in God's goodness and receive what He has already provided when He qualified you.

All your *disqualifications* exist in the *natural* realm. You live and operate in the *supernatural* (spiritual) realm where God has *qualified* you with His grace. God has fully qualified you in your born-again spirit. Remember, you are the righteousness of God in Christ Jesus.

Say out loud: "I am fully qualified to share in His inheritance!"

Let's summarize: Because of the finished work of Christ at Calvary, God has not credited, or imputed, sin against anyone for nearly 2,000 years. What God has imputed to you is "everlasting righteousness" (Dan. 9:24). Christ paid for all sins – past, present, and even future for every person for all time. The war is over. God is no longer angry because of your sin. Your sin is no longer an issue with God.

The war concerning your sin is over as far as heaven is concerned. This is such good news! The completeness of forgiveness is a truth that will transform you if you will receive the revelation of that forgiveness. You will view the Father in a different light -- as loving, gracious, and good.

Let's Discuss!

What are some of the ways you disqualify yourself from God's blessings?

How can you flip the script and walk in the truth that you are fully qualified in the eyes of your heavenly Father?

Let's Internalize and Apply!

1. Are the sins I commit an issue for God the Father? Why or why not?

____

____

2. When you were born again, how many of your sins were forgiven? Today, how many of your sins are forgiven? Which of your sins today are unforgiven?

____

____

3. Does God put a timeline on His forgiveness of your sins?

____

____

4. If you die as a Christian with unconfessed sin, do you go to heaven or hell?

____

____

Chapter 9

The Gift of a Good Conscience

But the goal of our instruction is love from a pure heart and a good conscience and a sincere faith. (1 Timothy 1:5)

One of the wonderful gifts that the Father has provided you through the finished work of Christ is the gift of a good conscience. In the verse above, the apostle Paul stated that having a good conscience and pure heart before God is foundational to walking in love and faith. If you don't have an accurate and upgraded conscience before God, then you will have a distorted and incomplete view of your true identity in Christ. This will interfere with your relationship with God – not feeling fully accepted by Him. You have already learned that you are totally accepted by the Father; let that truth be fully activated in your heart!

The apostles Paul and Peter declare the lack of a good conscience before God can negatively affect your relationship with others (1 Tim. 1:19; 1 Pet. 3:16). Not feeling fully accepted by the Father can open the door for feelings of rejection by others.

How do you develop a good conscience before God?

You develop a good conscience by having a scriptural understanding of two things: the completeness of your forgiveness by the Father (the previous chapter) and the gift of no condemnation.

Let's first learn about this wonderful gift of no condemnation and then what is required to have a good conscience.

God the Father has given you the *gift of no condemnation!*

> *Therefore, there is now no condemnation for those who are in Christ Jesus. . . Who is the one who condemns?* Romans 8:1, 34

God has given you the *gift of no condemnation*! The more you *believe* that you are righteous in Christ and *refuse to accept condemnation* for your past mistakes and present temptations, the more you will be set free from hindrances and addictions that bind you.

Even though you fail, there is no condemnation because you are in Christ and all your sins were washed away by His Blood. When God looks at you, He doesn't focus on your failures. God sees you as a *learner*, not a failure. As Jesus is spotless and without blame, so are you in your born-again spirit (the 'real' you)! Remember, as Jesus is now, so are you in this world (I John 4:17).

God sees you as a *learner*, not a failure.

Make this declaration out loud:

> I am *free from condemnation* because Jesus has given me the gift of no-condemnation!

If you feel condemned, it is not from God. Your own conscience may smite you, and Satan – the accuser of the brethren – may condemn you, but God does not.

When you do something wrong, you will sense a conviction from the Holy Spirit to repent of that sin. However, the feeling of condemnation is different – it's an *assault* against your sonship in Christ. That assault is either from Satan or your conscience, but it is not from God. Conviction from the Holy Spirit leads you to repentance and draws you into closer fellowship with the Lord; condemnation leads you to despair and hopelessness.

Condemnation does not come from the Godhead! Neither God the Father, nor Jesus, nor the Holy Spirit are condemning you (Romans 8:31-35). Your own heart may condemn you, and you may have blamed it on God. But God is *not* angry with you. God is not out to "get you." He is not even in a bad mood. God loves you! The Lord is truly at peace with you!

Condemnation is an *assault* against your sonship in Christ.

Remember, God the Father has given you the *gift of no condemnation*, which gives you the power to overcome your weaknesses and failures!

Let's look now at how to reject condemnation and develop a good conscience.

Condemnation Source #1: Our Adversary

> *No weapon that is formed against you will prosper; And every tongue that accuses you in judgment you will condemn. This is the heritage of the servants of the Lord, And their vindication* [righteousness] *is from Me, declares the Lord.* (Isaiah 54:17, bracket added)

We often quote this verse, but we should start at the end of the verse: you are declared righteous! That is an identity statement. Knowing that you are righteous in your born-again spirit enables you to confidently condemn and firmly reject every tongue of accusation, judgment, and condemnation that rises against you.

Action Step: Start speaking and maintaining your belief and confession that you are righteous. Use your faith for the most important thing -- believing that you are the righteousness of God in your spirit.

The adversary pours accusation on you using the *voice of a legalist* to disqualify you. (Because he is a legalist, you must repent, apply the blood of Christ, and declare in the courtroom of Heaven that you already have the gift of no condemnation!) He uses the voice of religion to accuse. Your adversary uses the law and commandments to show your failures, and to put a *spotlight on how your behavior has disqualified you* from fellowship with God, pointing out how undeserving you are of His acceptance, love, and blessings. He uses the law to heap condemnation upon you and give you a sense of guilt and distance from God. Your enemy knows that the more condemnation and guilt you experience, the more likely you are to feel alienated from God and continue in sin. (Remember, you are *fully qualified* to participate in His inheritance; embrace it!)

However, you should not allow the devil to condemn you for not keeping the Law; for the Law is for the unbeliever, and not for the righteous person.

> *But we know that the Law is good, if one uses it lawfully, realizing the fact <u>that law is not made for a righteous person</u>, but for those who are lawless and rebellious, for the ungodly and sinners, for the unholy and profane. . . (*I Timothy 1:8-9c)

If you will accept, believe, and rest in your Identity in Christ, and live and walk in the Holy Spirit, you will supernaturally keep, and even exceed, the requirements of the Law. Focusing on the law keeps you aware of sin. But focusing on righteousness by grace develops in you a righteousness consciousness -- which is how heaven views you!

The Litmus Test

The voice of accusation and condemnation only works if your adversary can get you to focus on *your* doing rather than *His* doing.

My Doing		His Doing
Self-occupied	vs:	Christ occupied
Self-conscious	vs:	Christ conscious
Me	vs:	my identity in Christ
My doing	vs:	Christ's doing/finished work

God is no shamer or fault-finder. He is no longer angry because of your sin!

Another Action Step: *Put the spotlight on the finished work of* Christ, who on the Cross took your condemnation and qualified you to receive God's acceptance, love, and favor forever!

Receive the gift of no condemnation, as it will give you the power to overcome your weaknesses and failures!

Condemnation Source #2: A conscience not fully transformed to a 'righteousness consciousness' belief system.

The second hinderance to a good conscience is the erroneous belief that your core self (your spirit) as a Christian is still sinful in some way. You still have a *sin-consciousness* rather than a *righteousness-consciousness.* Scripture calls this wrong view an *evil conscience.* Hebrews 10:22 records:

> *. . .let us draw near with a sincere heart in full assurance of faith, having our hearts sprinkled clean from an evil conscience. . .*

If you have an evil conscience, you still think that there are two versions of you: your new nature and your old nature. God only sees one version of you – the new man (Eph. 2:15; 4:24). You need to see the real you as having a *righteousness-consciousness,* which is how the Godhead sees you. Repent of continuing to believe that you have a sin-*consciousness* and embrace the real you – a *righteousness* version of you.

You will need to reprogram your conscience. Your conscience may have been programmed with a wrong belief system (from the old self or religion) based on dead works or an evil conscience, and needs to be upgraded. Make this declaration out loud:

> "I am as *righteous* and *holy, perfect* and *complete* as Jesus.

You need to embrace a *righteousness* view of who you are! Keep believing and declaring this over time and soon you will give your conscience a much-needed upgrade!

Let's Discuss!

When you sin, do you ever feel condemned? How should you respond?

What does it mean to have a "righteousness-consciousness?"

Let's Internalize and Apply!

1. When you feel condemned, what is/are the source(s)?

   ____

   ____

2. What are dead works? How do you cleanse your conscience of "dead works?"

   ____

   ____

3. What is meant by an "evil conscience?" What is the remedy for an evil conscience?

   ____

   ____

4. Will your born-again spirit be further "cleansed" when you get to heaven?

   ____

   ____

Chapter 10

"Give Me Back My Stuff!"

(An Application Process)

"Let us lay aside [renounce] *every weight,* [wrong perception]
*and the sin which so easily ensnares us. (*Heb. 12:1 NKJV, brackets added)

We have grown up in a world that is pretty negative. The world is inherently negative but the Kingdom isn't. Negatives are those things which are not a part of your new nature in Christ or the fruit of the Spirit. Negative thoughts and feelings manifest in such behaviors as anxiety and worry, fear, anger, doubt and unbelief, and frustration. There are no negative thoughts and feelings in heaven so we should not allow them in our mind or heart.

Negatives are a wrong perception about who you are. They are not how heaven perceives or views you. All negativity wars against your identity in Christ, against your sonship in Christ. Your biggest battles are always about your true identity.

All negativity wars against your identity in Christ, against your sonship in Christ.

Negativity and negative self-talk do not belong to you; they are not a part of your new man in Christ. Jesus paid dearly for them, therefore, they don't belong to you. They belong to Jesus, so put off these things and give them back to Jesus. He crucified and buried them for you, and He did not bring them through the resurrection. He only resurrected your new self in newness of life. Consider yourself dead to these negative things and remove them from your soul.

How do you get rid of negatives? First, you remove negatives by repenting of them. Be careful of the agreements that you make and speak. Second, invite Holy Spirit to help you keep your mind and heart in perfect peace by keeping your mind on the one true version of you – your new man.

Your biggest battles are always about your true identity.

The Duck and the Sponge

We each respond to negativity in different ways in differing situations. But we seem to have a propensity to respond in one of two ways.

You may be a person who tends to be a **sponge** as you respond to negativity. For example, someone may say something negative about you. As a sponge soaks up water, you respond by absorbing the negative thought and negative feeling associated with the negative comment. If you don't squeeze out that negative thought and feeling, you begin to adopt it as a part of your identity and act accordingly.

Or, you may be a person who generally responds to negativity like a **duck**. You don't seem to let negative thoughts bother you, as you let the thought and feeling associated with the negative comment run off "like water off of a duck's back."

Laurie speaking: *I have a melancholy temperament so I tend to absorb feelings of negativity like a sponge pretty easily. When I hear a negative statement made, I often absorb the feeling and the thinking that goes with it. Lon not so much, as he tends to respond to negativity like a duck. He doesn't seem to let negative thoughts bother him very much as he typically will not accept those words or feelings.*

Let's Discuss!

When it comes to responding to negativity, do you tend to respond like a sponge or like a duck?

Jesus Said, "Give Me Back My Stuff!"

We want to share a dream that Graham Cook shared about being caught up to heaven.[14]

Graham said that he had similar dreams as this one where Jesus was marching up a grassy hill with a smile on His face and was hugging others along the way. This time, Jesus was marching up the hill to him looking annoyed.

Jesus: *"Give me back my stuff!"*

Graham: "I don't know what you mean, Lord."

Jesus: *"Graham, don't mess with me. Give me back my stuff!"*

Graham: "I don't know what you mean."

Jesus: *"Sure you do. Give me back my stuff! I want it. And I want it right now!"*

Graham: "Jesus, I gave you everything. Honest."

---

[14] Graham Cooke, Jesus Demanded Graham Cooke, "Give Me Back My Stuff," https://www.youtube.com/watch?v=A-dBioGxk0E, July 7, 2014

Jesus: *"You took some stuff from me and I don't want you to have it. Now give it back to me."*

Graham: "I really don't know what you mean Lord."

Jesus: *"This is the last time. Give me back my stuff."*

Graham: "What stuff?"

Jesus: *"All that worry, that anger, that resentment, bitterness, fear. I died for it. I paid a price for it. It belongs to me. It doesn't belong to you. Give me back my stuff!"*

Graham: "Oh my God, I now get it. All those things You died for, You took them to the cross, and I've been resurrecting them. And I'm utterly appalled. I'm so sorry."

Jesus: *"Do you have any idea how delighted I was to die for all those things? When I was on the cross, it was the joy that was set before Me to die for all those things. On the cross, I knew that I was robbing you of experiencing all that negativity. I was taking all those things so that you would never have to experience them ever again. I can give you a whole new life where all those things are absent."*

"Do you know how excited I was to take all those things away from you – to never be fearful again, or worried or panicked? To never have to be angry, or bitter or resentful? To never have to do any of that stuff again? You can be free of all negativity."

"All your negative ways of looking at things that make you cynical and sarcastic. All your negative ways of seeing or thinking. Ways that make you imagine the worst before seeing the best."

"I robbed you of all that negativity so you can <u>see</u> the best, <u>think</u> the best, <u>believe</u> the best, and <u>be</u> the best."

"And you keep taking it all back, like it belongs to you. It doesn't belong to you. I died for it. I paid a price for it. It's mine. Give Me back my stuff. You can't have it."

"All the time you are taking hold of these things, you can't see who you really are in Me. You can't be the person I see when I look at you. Every time you take up all those things, there is a disconnect between you and heaven. I died so that you could stay connected with heaven. It's called, abiding – staying, remaining in that place in Me." Then you can have My accelerated goodness, My grace, My power."

My son, I want my stuff back. You and I have important things to do."

End of dream.

When Graham awoke from the dream, he said he wrote down all the things he had taken from Jesus. Next to those things he wrote all the positive things that were the opposite of those negative things. He turned each negative into a positive and began living from his true identity in Christ and manifesting the fruit of the Spirit.

Let's Discuss!

What things have you taken from Jesus that He died for?

What do you need to repent of and give back to Him?

How can you replace those things with the fruit of the Spirit in your life?

Making War on Negativity

Negativity is not a part of your identity in Christ.

Every negative, whether anxiety, worry, fear, doubt, or frustration, becomes a weight that hinders the free manifestation of your true identity in Christ (Heb. 12:1). You are to lay aside every weight, all negativity which so easily entangles you. They don't belong to you. They are not a part of your true identity in Christ.

- All negativity is an assault against your identity in Christ.
- Negatives distract you from your true identity and destiny.
- Negatives can distort how you perceive who you really are in Christ.
- Negatives challenge the truths God has declared about you.

All negativity is an assault against your identity in Christ.

You may know from experience that negativity leads to wrong perceptions about God and about yourself, and manifests as negative behavior, negative thinking, negative emotions, sarcasm, and cynicism. However, the Holy Spirit wants to expose the lies of negativity about your true identity and wants to correct how you *see* yourself, *think* about yourself, and *talk* about yourself.

All of your negatives have already been addressed at the Cross.

Here's the good news! All negatives were crucified and buried in Christ with our sins. Negativity is a part of the old man, not the new man.

The shed blood of Christ has already paid for all negatives in your life. They don't belong to you. Our perspective needs to be:

> If it doesn't exist in heaven, it can't exist here.
>
> If it is not in Christ, you don't want it. Don't accept it.

A negative is a weight that was crucified and buried in Christ along with your sins. Let your sin and all negativity, buried with Christ, remain in the grave.

When you are weary and heavy-laden -- with all your negative attachments, negative thinking, negative emotions -- Jesus directs you to come to Him and give Him your negatives. He will give you rest. He invites you to take His yoke and learn from Him (Matt. 11:28-30). When you do, His yoke is easy and light because there are no negatives attached to it. Consider yourself dead to all negativity and give it back to Jesus. His yoke does not contain any negativity.

Negativity presses against your born-again spirit and your walk in the Spirit.

Negatives press against your walk in the Spirit and the full expression of the fruit of the Spirit. The lies of all negatives press against and challenge:

- your *perception* of what's true in your born-again spirit, (which is as righteous, complete, and perfect as Jesus is now)

- how you *think* and *feel* about yourself, and
- how you *talk* about yourself.

Negatives will seek to restrict, frustrate, or even nullify the flow of God's grace in your life (Gal. 2:21). Since you are crucified with Christ, and your old nature is in the grave, don't let negativity arise to frustrate the flow of the grace of God in your life.

Think of a negative as a way of life that is taught by the flesh, the world and religion. A negative can become a behavior pattern, a way of thinking or feeling that is unhelpful. A negative is a thought or feeling you have *given consent to* that can never produce His fullness of life in you. You now have a consensual relationship with that negative and you must come out of agreement with it.

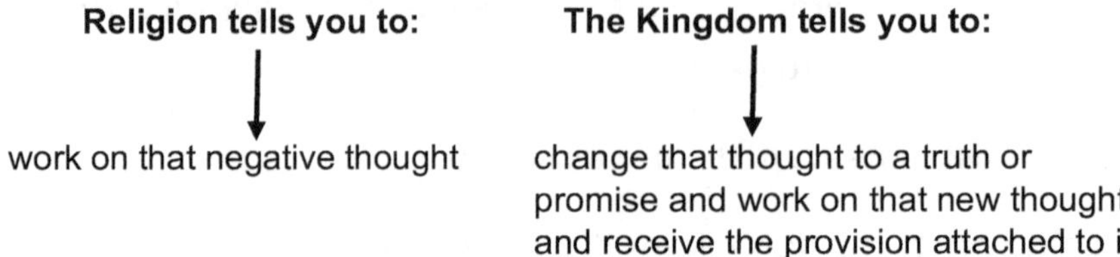

For example, religion tells you to work on your negative thought, say worry. On the other hand, the Kingdom tells you not to think about worry, but to change it into a promise such as, "cast all your anxieties on Him, because He cares for you" (1 Pet. 5:7). Work on that instead and receive God's provision of rest attached to it. Give Jesus back your worries – about life, about tomorrow, about what you eat, drink, or wear. These worries don't belong to you.

The Kingdom never works on a negative (using behavior modification); rather, Holy Spirit works *within* you by prompting you to change that negative thought into a truth about your identity, and He works on that thought. Holy Spirit seeks to convert the negative or wrong perception into something that is true about the new man so He can deal with it. The Godhead only works on your new man, never the old. God only speaks to you from your identity in Christ. The Lord refuses to work with a negative because there are no negatives in heaven.

Let's do what 1 Peter 5:7 instructs us to do, *"casting all your anxiety on Him, because He cares for you."* The word "anxiety" in the Greek is *merimna,* which means "to divide and fracture a person's being into parts." Anxiety (cares, worries) draws you away from the main thing, which is to be single minded about who you are in Christ. If you become mentally preoccupied on the negatives, you will lock in and become double-minded – a person of two minds (James 1:8). The scripture records, *"I hate those who are double-minded" (Ps. 119:113).* So, give Jesus back His stuff – all the negatives in its various forms – and walk single-focused on your new man in Christ!

Application Steps

Follow these four steps to give your negatives back to Jesus:

STEP 1: Identity all the negatives that you are holding onto that are not a part of your new nature in Christ. They may be negative thoughts, feelings, and behavior. Examples: anxieties, worries, doubts and unbelief, fears, frustrations, sarcasm, or cynicism.

STEP 2: In prayer, give each negative thought/feeling/behavior back to Jesus. Remember, negatives are part of the old nature that do not belong to you. You must *come out of consensual agreement* with each negative. Jesus will give you rest, so accept His invitation to take His yoke and learn from Him because His yoke does not contain any negativity.

STEP 3: For each negative, identify an opposite positive that God has declared about you in His Word. These positives will include truths, identity statements, or fruit of the Spirit that are a part of your new man. Consider yourself dead to all negativity and give it back to Jesus.

STEP 4: Declare/confess each positive daily or several times each day, especially when you discern a negative is trying to re-surface in your life.

Let's Internalize and Apply!

1. T/F All negativity is at war against your identity or sonship in Christ.

2. Are negativity and negative self-talk a part of your new man in Christ?

   ____

   ____

3. When Jesus says to give Him back His stuff, what does He want returned?

   ____

   ____

4. In what four ways does negativity war against your true identity in Christ?

____

____

5. In what three areas does negativity press against your born-again spirit?

____

____

6. Negativity can be thought of as an attachment or weight to your life that comes from what three sources?

____

____

7. What does the kingdom of God tell you to focus on regarding a negative thought? How does this differ from what religion tells you to do?

____

____

8. T/F The Lord refuses to work with a negative because there are no negatives in heaven.

Section 3

The Role of Faith

As you learned in the previous section, the outcome from repenting of dead works -- your efforts to gain the Father's love and acceptance – is to gain a clear conscience before God. You have repented of your efforts and called upon the blood of Christ to cleanse you in the courts of Heaven.

We now move on to the next principle – *faith toward God.* The outcome of the *faith in God* principle is that you graduate from having a sin-consciousness view of yourself, and embrace a *righteousness consciousness* view of yourself. After all, this is the only version that Father God has of you as the new man in Christ.

In Chapter 11, you will learn what it means to have faith in God. In Chapter 12, you will learn the importance of developing a righteousness view of yourself. Finally, in Chapter 13, you will learn a practical process to remove the sin-consciousness view and replace it with the desired view of righteous-consciousness.

Chapter 11

Faith in God

We come now to the second principle: *faith in God.* This second principle is intertwined with the first principle of *repentance from dead works* in the context of the courts of Heaven. Think of these first two principles as two complementary sides of a coin.

Let's recap who and what speaks for you in the courts of Heaven. First, the Father, who is the Judge of all, is on your side. How do you know? He delivered up his Son for you (Rom. 8:31-32)! Second, Jesus is for you. He died for you and shed His blood for you. Jesus is now at the right hand of the Father always interceding for you as your advocate and defense attorney.[15] You have the best lawyer and Advocate – Jesus! And better yet, His Father is the Judge. The odds are in your favor with this Judge and your defense attorney.

Furthermore, Jesus' shed blood *"speaks better things"* about you in the courts of Heaven before the Judge of all (Heb. 12:24). The blood of Jesus answers every accusation against you, cleansing your conscience of dead works and an evil conscience (removing the old version of you so you can focus exclusively on your new nature). With both the Father and Jesus rooting for you, you cannot lose!

As you learned in the previous section, scripture uses courtroom language to describe the receiving of salvation. Repentance from dead works occurs in the spirit realm in the court of Heaven, resulting in your forgiveness. Your belief and acceptance of the finished work of Christ (death, burial, resurrection, and seating in heaven) for your salvation is also recognized in the courts of Heaven. This expression of your faith in God is referred to as the *doctrine of justification*.

The Two-fold Work of Christ

Understanding the doctrine of justification includes three biblical or theological terms: redemption, propitiation, and justification. The doctrine of justification is often represented as a triangle, called The Salvation Triangle.

---

[15] Romans 8:34; Hebrews 7:25

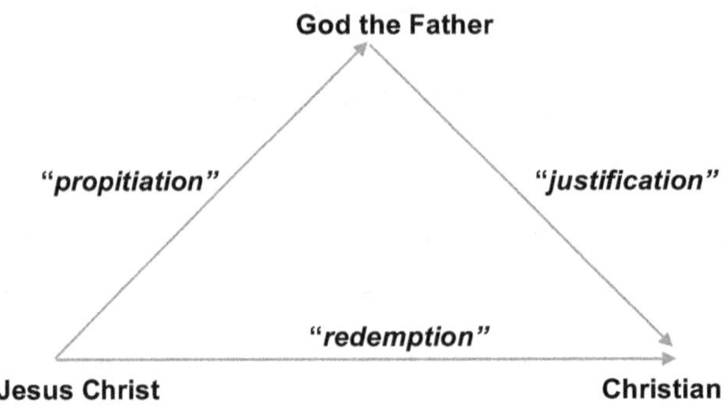

Notice that God justifies you based on the two-fold work of Christ. First, along the bottom of the triangle, Christ rescued you from sin by *redeeming* you: *"you were redeemed with. . . the precious blood of Christ* (I Pet. 1:18-19). Jesus redeemed you by purchasing you with His own blood. This is what *He did* for you, not what you *could do* for yourself.

Second, along the left side of the triangle, Jesus satisfied the Father's righteous anger, wrath, and fiery indignation against all of your sins.[16] He turned aside the Father's wrath forever (known as *propitiation*) through His sacrificial death. This is what Jesus did for you in relation to the Father. The apostle John writes of this work of Christ:

> *If anyone sins, we have an Advocate with the Father, Jesus Christ the righteous; and He Himself is the* <u>*propitiation*</u> *for our sins; and not for ours only, but also for those of the whole world.* (I John 2:1b – 2).

God the Father was fully satisfied with the payment of His Son on the cross and will never be angry with you about your sin. When it was completed, Jesus shouted, "It is finished!" Jesus permanently turned aside God's wrath, anger, and fury against your sin through his sacrifice of atonement.

So Jesus made a double payment – *redemption* and *propitiation* -- for all sins for all time, taking the full brunt of the punishment you deserved, satisfying God's justice (Is. 40:2). The apostle Paul wrote that the finished work of Christ made us *"one new man"* when He reconciled us to the Father (Eph. 2:15-16). Now, God is in total peace with you because the full payment for your sin was completed nearly 2000 years ago!

Lon speaking: *I've always understood that Jesus redeemed me as a result of His work on the Cross, but I did not understand His propitiatory work. When I committed a sin, I*

---

[16] See Isaiah 53:10-11; 54:9-10

wrongly thought that if I did not quickly repent, God would be angry with me. As a result, I was not fully trusting the Father since I was sure that "the other shoe was going to drop" on me because of a sin for which I had not repented. I did not understand that Jesus took the full brunt of the Father's anger toward my sin and now if I do sin, it does not separate me from the Lord. Now I know God is in total peace with me. The war is over!

The good news is that on the basis of Christ's *redemptive* and *propitiatory* work, God is right in *justifying* you (along the right side of the triangle). In the courts of Heaven, you now can freely remind the Judge that the shed blood of Christ speaks better things of you. All of your sins – past, present, and future - have been fully paid!

God's *holiness* is now on your side. His *righteousness* is now for you, not against you. You are His beloved in whom He is well pleased because of Jesus' finished work. He is delighted with you.

Summary of Justification

Justification, then, is heaven's decision *for* you that is rendered by the *"Judge of all,"* based on the two-fold work of Christ of redemption and propitiation. Picture the Father's verdict where He justifies you in the courts of Heaven. Jesus took all of the guilt and punishment that you should have received and He gave to you His righteousness instead. The scriptural foundation for the doctrine of justification transpiring in the courts of Heaven is captured in these verses:

> *Therefore, having been justified by faith, we have peace with God through our Lord Jesus Christ, through whom also we have obtained our introduction by faith into this grace in which we stand.* (Romans 5:1-2)
>
> *For by grace you have been saved through faith; and that not of yourselves, it is the gift of God; not as a result of works, so that no one may boast.* (Ephesians 2:8-9)

How do you obtain and walk in justification?

First, repent of your dead works as a way to gain God's acceptance. Forsake this approach so you can walk in a position of justification before God (the *Repentance from Dead Works* Principle).

If we confess our sins, He is faithful and righteous to forgive us our sins and to cleanse of from all righteousness. (I John 1:9)

Second, accept Jesus Christ as your satisfactory payment for sin through faith in His blood and gain the status of justified (the *Faith in God* Principle). Romans 3:24 – 25 summarizes the entire doctrine of justification when it states:

> *Being justified as a gift by His grace through redemption which is in Christ Jesus; whom God displayed publicly as a propitiation in His blood through faith.* (Romans 3:24-25)

Finally, believe that God has accepted your repentance and faith in Christ Jesus, making you His child. *For you are all sons of God through faith in Christ Jesus"* (Gal. 3:26).

The ultimate goal of fully accepting and implementing the *faith in God* principle is for you to adopt a *righteousness* view of yourself. You stop seeing yourself as a sinner (with a sin consciousness) but rightly see yourself as a righteous saint. A *saint* is one who is recognized as holy through the blood of Christ in the courts of Heaven. You can honestly and genuinely say:

> "I no longer see myself as a sinner, but as a saint. . . who occasionally sins."

Yes, you will occasionally sin, and when you do, Holy Spirit will convict you. You will sense this in your conscience. Confess this sin and ask Him to cleanse you with His precious blood. The blood of Christ is all the evidence you need to present to the Judge of all to obtain a verdict of forgiveness. In so doing, you continue in right standing with the Judge of all in the courts of Heaven. Begin to see yourself as a *saint*, and not a *sinner.* A 'righteousness consciousness' is the gold standard you are to pursue.

I am a saint. . . who occasionally sins."

Let's Internalize and Apply!

1. Who is for you in the courts of Heaven?

   ____

   ____

2. What speaks loudly on your behalf in the courts of Heaven?

   ____

   ____

3. True/False: Faith in God is your belief and acceptance of the finished work of Christ for your salvation that is recognized in the courts of Heaven.

4. What is meant by the two-fold work of Christ?

   ____

   ____

5. True/False: The ultimate goal of fully accepting and implementing the *faith in God* principle is for you to adopt a *sin-consciousness* view of yourself.

6. True/False: You can genuinely say, "I no longer see myself as a sinner, but as a saint. . . who occasionally sins.

Chapter 12

Developing A Righteousness Consciousness

The outcome of the *faith in God* principle is that you no longer live life from a sin-consciousness view of yourself, but from a *righteousness-consciousness* view. God does not have a *sin consciousness* view of you, because Jesus dealt with your sin once and for all. Rather, the Godhead has a *righteousness conscious*ness or view of you made in Their image and likeness. In fact, it was the Father's desire that you have *"no more consciousness of sin,"* because that is not your new identity (Heb. 10:2).

The Lord is working to remove a 'sin-consciousness' view from you and replace it with a 'righteousness consciousness' view. This is the only way your Father sees you and works with you. The Father, Jesus, and Holy Spirit only see one version of you, as a new man or creation in Christ. God only speaks to you in line with your identity in Christ. Let's learn how you can partner with Him in this transforming process.

The New Testament idea of *confess* simply means "to agree and say what God says." When you "confess," you are releasing testimony in the courts of Heaven that agrees with what the Father declares about you. One practical approach we recommend is for you to say what God says about you by declaring the *"You Saids."* Talk about yourself – the 'real' you -- the way God sees you and talks about you in His Word. For example, you can declare:

"Heavenly Father, ***You said***:

> I am the righteousness of God in Christ Jesus.
>
> I am completely forgiven of all my sins."
>
> I am complete, perfect, and holy as Jesus is.

The Father loves it when you speak His Word back to Him. Make it an on-going practice to believe, speak, and activate all that God believes and thinks about you.

Below you will find truth statements about you that reflect how your true identity is recognized in the courts of Heaven. Your identity in Christ consists of truth statements, each reflecting a unique facet of who you are as a *new man* in Christ. These truth statements fall into three clusters: I am Accepted, I am Secure, and I am Significant.

Declaring these truths releases testimony in the courts of Heaven on your behalf. It is a robust way to implement the *faith in God* principle.

I am Accepted

The identity statements below focus on your **acceptance** in Christ.

"Father, I believe and confess these truths about me. *You said*:"

- I am *totally accepted* by God (Rom. 15:7; Eph. 1:5-6 NKJV); to the extent that the Father accepted the finished work of Jesus, He accepts me
- I am *reconciled* to God and *adopted* as His child (Rom. 5:11; Eph. 1:5)
- I am *chosen* by God, holy and dearly loved (Col. 3:12; I Pet. 2:9)
- I am *well pleasing* to God (Matt. 3:17; Mark 1:11); I am in Christ who was well-pleasing to His Father
- I am *approved by God* (I Thess. 2:4)
- I am a *friend* of God (John 15:15)
- I am *completely forgiven* of all of my sins – past, present, and future (I John 2:1-2; Col. 3:13; Heb. 9:12, 15; 10:10, 14)
- I am *free from condemnation* because Jesus has given me the gift of no-condemnation (Rom. 8:1, 34).
- I am the *righteousness of God* in Christ Jesus (Eph. 4:24; II Cor. 5:21).
- I am *holy* and without blame before God (Eph. 4:24; I Cor. 3:17; I Pet. 2:5, 9)
- I am *perfect, complete, and mature* as Jesus (Heb. 10:14; 12:23)
- I am a *new creation* in Christ and therefore a 3rd heaven creation. (II Cor. 5:17-18; Gal. 6:15)
- I am a *partaker of His divine nature* (2 Pet. 1:4)
- I am a *saint* (a "holy one") (Eph. 2:19; Rom. 1:7; Col. 1:2)
- I am a *masterpiece* (His "workmanship") (Eph. 2:10)
- I am *crowned* with *glory* and *honor* (Heb. 2:7)

- I am a *child* of the Most High God! (John 1:12; Rom. 8:16)
- I am *fully qualified* to share in the fullness of His inheritance (Col. 1:12).
- I am *redeemed* from the curse of the law, *purchased* by God (Gal. 3:13; I Pet. 1:18-19; I Cor. 6:19-20; Acts 20:28)
- I am *deeply and tenderly loved* by God (John 3:16; Jer. 31:3)
- I am *highly favored* (Eph. 1:6; Luke 1:28); in fact, I am *crowned with favor* (Prov. 4:9)
- I am *greatly blessed* and cannot be cursed (Eph. 1:3; Numb. 23:8, 20)
- I am a *joint heir* with Christ, sharing His inheritance with Him (Rom. 8:17)
- *I am sanctified* (positionally) as holy to God *(Heb. 2:11)*
- I am *fearfully* and *wonderfully made* (Psalm 139:14)
- I am a member of a *chosen race*, a *royal priesthood*, a *holy nation* (I Pet. 2:9-10)
- I am *justified* (declared not guilty) by the Blood of Christ (Rom. 5:9)
- I am a *victor*, not a victim. I have the *victory* through the Lord Jesus Christ (I Cor. 15:57)

I am Secure

The identity statements below focus on your **security** in Christ.

"Father, I believe and confess these truths about me". *"You said:"*

- I am *hidden with Christ* in God (Col. 3:3)
- I am *born again* and the evil one cannot touch me (I John 5:18).
- I am a *temple* in which God dwells (I Cor. 3:16)
- I am *united* to the Lord, one spirit with Him (I Cor. 6:17)
- I am *firmly rooted* and built up in Christ (Col. 2:7)
- I am a *living stone*, being built up in Christ as a spiritual house (I Pet. 2:5)
- I *cannot be separated* from the love of God (Rom. 8:35)
- I am securely *established* and *sealed* by God (2 Cor. 1:21, 22)

- I am *assured* that all things are working together for good (Rom. 8:28)
- I am a *citizen of heaven* (Phil. 3:20)
- I am *confident* that the *good work* God has begun in me *will be completed* (Phil. 1:6)
- I am the *head* and not the tail; I am *above only* and not beneath (Deut. 28:13)
- I am co-*crucified, co-buried, co-resurrected, co-ascended,* and *co-seated with Christ* in the heavenly realm and have 3rd heaven authority.
- I am *strong in the Lord* and in the strength of His might. (Eph. 6:10)

I have Significance

The identity statements below focus on your **significance** in Christ.

"Father, I believe and confess these truths about me". *"You said:"*

- I am *salt* and *light* in the world (Matt. 5:13-14)
- I am a *child of light* (Matt. 5:14: I Thess. 5:5)
- I am a *branch* of Christ's vine, a channel of His life (John 15:1, 5)
- I am a *member* of Christ's body (I Cor. 12:27)
- I am God's *coworker* (2 Cor. 6:1; I Cor. 3:9)
- I am *chosen* and *appointed* to *bear fruit* (John 15:16)
- I am a *minister* of reconciliation (2 Cor. 5:17 – 20)
- I am an *ambassador* of Christ (II Cor. 5:20)
- I am *more than a conqueror* (Rom. 8:37)
- I am *called* of God to fulfill my divine destiny (2 Tim. 1:9)
- I am a *king* and *priest* unto God (Rev. 1:6; 5:10)
- I am *transformed* from glory to glory into God's glory (2 Cor. 3:18)

Chapter 13

Putting Off, Putting On

(An Application Process)

We want to share with you a very simple way to apply *repentance from dead works* and *faith in God* – as one process. The process is called the Recirculting Process.

Let's revisit Ephesians 4:22-25 which you learned about previously:

> *. . .lay aside the old self. . . and that you be renewed in the spirit of your mind, and put on the new self* [Greek anthropos = new man], *which in the likeness of God has been created in righteousness and holiness of the truth. Therefore, laying aside falsehood* [pseudo], *speak truth. . .*

Paul uses the language of putting off and putting on. It is the picture of *changing clothes.* As believers and followers of Jesus, we are to make sure we have the right clothing on before Him as we engage in the courts of Heaven. Just like in the natural, we do not put on one set of clothes over another, so we don't do this in the spirit. We must *undress to redress.* In other words, we must *put off* the old man and his deeds. The *old man* is the old nature whose desires are against God and His ways. When you were born-again, this *old man* died and was left buried in the grave. Consider yourself dead to sin and alive to God. The Father does.

Even though the old nature was crucified and left in the grave, we still have a mind that needs to be transformed by the Holy Spirit and the Word. Our mind and heart still retain a lot of wrong thinking about who God is, about our identity in Christ, and negative thoughts about ourselves -- all beliefs that carried over from our old nature. Our born-again spirit has been fully transformed but our soul has not. So our soul (mind, heart) must catch up to what has already transpired in our spirit. Putting off these wrong ways of thinking is like changing a set of clothes. In our mind, we must crucify the old and resurrect the new.

As a result of the *old man* dying, we must discard the ways of the old nature by actively renouncing and rejecting the old. The new nature in our spirit prompts us to love what God loves and to hate what God hates. We are now free to bring our behavior into agreement with God's nature and ways.

The Recircuiting process we are about to share is a *putting off* and a *putting on.* Here are important elements of the recircuiting process.

PUT OFF the imposter: Put off (that is, crucify) the falsehood (*pseudos* = lies, imposter, fake) notions of who you are. This means to *renounce* and *reject* them as not who you are. This is the repenting phase.

- *Actively* renounce and reject, and cut all ties with each false notion. Put them to death.

- *Root out* entrenched habits (i.e., critical words, quick to anger, tendency to be fearful).

If you have a deep-seated wound in your spirit from a prior experience that resulted in a vivid negative memory, you will need to *aggressively* root out that memory and replace it with the truth about your identity in Christ. This can be especially challenging if there is a strong emotional attachment associated with that memory.

Put off wrong hearing – labels, lies.

Put off wrong believing, feelings and attitudes.

Put off wrong speaking – negative self-talk.

Put off wrong habits and practices.

In doing so, you are removing inaccurate perceptions, wrong beliefs, agreements, and attachments from your soul.

> Mistakes, labels from others, wrong attitudes, and negative self-talk do not belong to you. . . they belong to Jesus.

Your mistakes, labels from others, wrong attitudes, and negative self-talk do not belong to you. Jesus paid dearly for them, so they don't belong to you. They belong to Jesus, so put off these things and give them back to Him. He crucified and buried them for you, and He did not bring them through the resurrection. He only resurrected your new self which was raised in newness of life. Consider yourself dead to these negative things. In the future, be careful of the agreements that you consent to and speak.

Let's Discuss!

What are those things in your mind that you need to reject, renounce, and cut out?

What do you need to "put to death?"

The Father only sees one version of you – your new man. Your old self was crucified at the cross. Let's pray and reinforce this truth in the courts of Heaven:

> *Lord Jesus, as I stand before Your Courts, I thank You that the old man has died with You at the cross. When You died on the cross, the old man / old nature in me died with You. I now by faith discard this old man way of thinking like a set of unwanted clothes. The passions and desires associated with that old nature no longer have control over me. Thank You, Lord Jesus, that You now empower me to be clothed with the newness of Your nature and life. Amen!*

RENEW: To renew means to relearn. Actively renew your mind with the truth of who you are in your born-again spirit as found in the Word of God.[17] Renewing your mind in this manner implants the truth into your heart to replace the false.

PUT ON more of Your New Self: Speak out-loud what is true about you and the life within you. In faith, actively *announce*, *confess*, and *embrace* out-loud the truth about your identity in Christ. This is like *receiving* and being *fully clothed* with a new garment. As you do, the Father is UPGRADING you on the inside, taking you up higher into your identity.

Put on right hearing – based on your true identity in Christ.

Put on right believing and attitudes.

Put on right speaking – positive self-talk.

Put on right habits and a righteous lifestyle.

Now, you are believing right and making good agreements and attachments to your soul.

> The Father is UPGRADING you on the inside, taking you up higher into your identity.

Clothed to Stand in His Courts

To operate as a priest before the Lord in His courts, you must wear the right clothes. Clothing is important in the spirit realm. We all are "wearing" something in the spirit realm. To function in the courts of Heaven requires the right attire.

---

17 Ephesians 4:23 "*be renewed in the spirit of your mind. . .*"; Romans 12:2 "*be transformed by the renewing of your mind. .*"

Endeavor to be clothed with the "right garments" so you are recognized in the spirit world as one who can function there. We as kings and priests of our God are to have the right clothing for this function (Rev. 5:10). As we repent and stand before the Lord, His blood will cause us to have on the right garments, so that we may stand in His presence without fear and operate as His priests in His Courts.

You clothed yourself with the nature of Christ when you embraced a righteousness-consciousness view of yourself; you possess His divine nature (2 Pet. 1:3-4) to operate in the courts of Heaven. You must make sure that your thoughts and actions are in agreement with the new nature you have received.

Let's pray to put on the right clothes:

> *Lord, as I stand in Your Courts, I ask that I might be clothed with Your divine nature. I ask that I would be clothed with a robe of righteousness that would allow me to function as a king and priest before You in the spirit realm. Lord, take away any negativity and shame associated with me, and allow me to stand before You completely welcomed and recognized as Your son/daughter. I thank you that I stand before you accepted and pleasing to You as the result of the finished work of Christ. I am now clothed with the right garments provided for me through Your atoning blood. Amen!*

Let's Discuss!

What are some ways that you can form the new man in your mind and heart?

As a Christian, the spiritual realm recognizes who you are in Christ and what you carry. Heaven certainly does. The forces of darkness know who you are in Christ and the anointing you carry, which is why they fear you. Make it your aim to know who you are in Christ.

The Recircuiting Steps

Now let's implement the simple steps of *recircuiting* your mind. The first step is DIAGNOSIS. Ask the Lord two questions concerning the lies and truths regarding your identity. Take the time to listen to what the Lord says to you and write them down.

> What **lies** do I believe about my identity that I need to change?
>
> What's **true** about my identity?

Once you have answers and scriptures from the Lord, move on to the final step: the CURE.

For each lie about your true identity, you must repent, reject and renounce and then declare or announce what is really true from scripture. In so doing, you are making a new agreement.

Recircuiting Steps

DIAGNOSIS	CURE / REWIRING
Ask God 2 questions:	(*making new neuro-connections*)
What **LIES** do I believe about [my identity]? (failure, disappointed God, feel unworthy, etc.)	I **reject and renounce** the lie that ______.
What's **TRUE** about [my identity]? (success, God is proud of me, not disappointed in me)	I choose to believe and **declare and announce** that _____________.
	(*making new agreements*)

Now, you have intentionally made a new agreement in your mind and in faith you speak words of the new agreement into the spiritual realm and the physical realm. This sends a signal to your sub-conscious mind which begins to dissolve the negative neuropath (wrong belief) and begins to build the new neuropath. Choose to make only positive agreements with your words and mind.

This process physically recodes or rewires your brain. With the words of your new agreement, you are partnering with God to recode your thinking and feelings, which drives your actions, which then drives the new result (beliefs about yourself).

Let's Discuss!

Returning to the two question to ask God:

*What are the **lies**, wrong perceptions, and negativity that I have believed and agreed to that need to be renounced and rejected?*

*What is the **truth** about my identity that I need to embrace and declare that results in a new agreement and attachment?*

Examples

Let's look at examples of the recircuiting steps in action. Here is the first example.

From ***I Feel Rejected. . .*** to ***God Deeply Loves and Totally Accepts Me!***

Romans 15:7

Therefore, accept one another, just as Christ also accepted us to the glory of God.

Romans 5:5

The love of God has been poured out within our hearts through the Holy Spirit who was given to us.

I REPENT and RENOUNCE the lie that I am rejected, and ANNOUNCE the truth that God deeply loves me and He totally accepts me!

I declare that I am deeply loved by God!

I declare that I am totally accepted and fully pleasing to God!

From ***I Feel Depressed. . .*** to ***God Has Provided Me with Peace and Joy!***

Philippians 4:4

Rejoice in the Lord always; again I will say, rejoice!

Philippians 4:7

And the peace of God, which surpasses all comprehension, will guard your hearts and your minds in Christ Jesus.

Romans 15:13

Now may the God of hope fill you with all joy and peace in believing, so that you will abound in hope by the power of the Holy Spirit.

I REPENT and RENOUNCE all feelings of depression, and ANNOUNCE the truth that God has provided me with peace and joy!

I declare that I will rejoice in the Lord continually!

I declare that I choose to live a life filled with joy!

I declare that I have the peace of God which passes all understanding!

From ***My Future Seems Bleak. . .*** to ***God Has a Great Plan for My Life!***

Psalm 139:14, 16

I am fearfully and wonderfully made.

In Your book were all written the days that were ordained for me.

Jeremiah 29:11, 13

'For I know the plans that I have for you,' declares the Lord, 'plans for welfare and not for calamity to give you a future and a hope.' You will seek Me and find Me when you search for Me with all your heart.

Acts 13:36

For David. . . served the purpose of God in his own generation.

I REPENT and RENOUNCE the lie that God has a bleak future for me, and ANNOUNCE the truth that God is absolutely good and has a great plan and destiny for my life!

I declare that my destiny which You have written in Your destiny book about me in heaven will come to pass!

I choose to connect to my destiny!

I declare that Father God is absolutely good and has a good plan for my life!

I decree that I will fulfill my God-given destiny and assignment in this season!

I decree that I will serve and fulfill the purposes of God in my generation!

Let's Internalize and Apply!

1. In the Recircuiting steps, what are the two questions to ask the Lord in the Diagnosis step?

   ____

   ____

2. What are the two phases of the Cure (or Rewiring) step?

   ____

   ____

Section 4

Toward Maturity

"Therefore, leaving the discussion of the elementary principles of Christ, let us go on to perfection. . ." (Heb. 6:1a NKJV). The word *perfection* in this verse means mature or complete. The end-goal of learning how the Father sees and knows you is to be a mature and complete son or daughter in Christ.

We devote the last chapter of this book to describe what it means to be a mature son or daughter. Certainly it means to understand and apply the principles of not laying again the foundation of repentance from dead works and of faith in God. But being mature in the Hebrews 6:1 sense means that you come to the level of being "adopted as a son." What does that really mean? Let's unpack this important perspective.

Chapter 14

Becoming a Mature Son

"let us go on to perfection. . . Hebrews 6:1

God wants all of His children to grow up and become mature sons and daughters. The process of maturing is both an invitation and an expectation. Our initial thought may be that to *"go on to perfection"* in this life is not possible. But let's understand how the word "perfection" is being used here. The word *perfection* in Hebrews 6:1 means a state of being mature or complete.

A fully mature person possesses full authority to represent the family name and business. This person is authorized to speak and represent the father in all matters. In the context of the Kingdom of God, a mature person is certainly one who mastered the six principles or foundation stones that comprised the apostles' doctrine. But there is more to being a mature son or daughter.

As a mature person, you also:

- are skilled to teach the word of righteousness
- are able to discern between good and evil
- know God's voice and ways because you are led by Holy Spirit.
- are skilled enough to partake of the meat (solid food) in God's word, and
- know how to use the keys of kingdom authority on behalf of King Jesus.

In your journey to become a mature "son", let's look in scripture at four Greek words for a daughter or son, each depicting a different level of maturity. These words are used to describe various stages of spiritual maturity. Let's do a little vocabulary work. (We are not seeking to overwhelm you with Greek vocabulary but to give you the right perspective!)

- *Nepios* means "no speech" and refers to an infant or baby and appear in these scriptures: 1 Corinthians 3:1 says: *"And I, brethren, could not speak to you as to spiritual men, but as to men of flesh, as to infants in Christ."*

- A *paidion* is a toddler or young child; Matthew 18:4 says, *"Whoever then humbles himself as this child, he is the greatest in the kingdom of heaven."*

- A *teknon* is a child, up to and including a teenager or young adult; immature. Galatians 4:19 says, *"My children, with whom I am again in labor until Christ is formed in you."* 1 John 5:21, *"Little children, guard yourselves from idols."*

- Finally, a *huios* is a fully matured "son." Romans 8:14 says, *"For all who are being led by the Spirit of God, these are sons of God."* Matthew 5:45, *"...so that you may be sons of your Father who is in heaven. . ."*

The last term, *huios*, is the goal the Lord is seeking. Spiritually speaking, *huios* is not a gender term; just as a male can be part of Christ's "bride," females can be a fully mature "son." (In a similar way, Jesus made us a new "man" (*anthropos)* in Ephesians 2:15, which also is not referring to gender, but to mankind or the human race; *anthropos* includes both women and men created in the image of God.)

The Peril of Not Advancing

The audience of the book of Hebrews was learning about the peril of not advancing to maturity as believers. From the tone of the passage in Hebrews 5, the writer seems to be issuing a rebuke to his audience. Hebrews 5:12 – 14 NKJV reads:

> *For though by this time you ought to be teachers* [didaskalos = master], *you need someone to teach you again the first principles of the oracles of God; and you have come to need milk and not solid food.*
>
> *For everyone who partakes only of milk is unskilled* [apeiros = inexperienced] *in the word of righteousness, for he is a babe* [nepios = infant, simple-minded].
>
> *But solid food belongs to those who are of full age* [teleious = mature, full-grown], *that is, those who by reason of use have their senses exercised to discern both good and evil.*

Let this passage be an exhortation to you to step up your growth into spiritual adulthood.

The writer of Hebrews (perhaps the apostle Paul?) uses the analogy of those not advancing in their understanding and skill as ones still needing milk and not ready for solid food. The audience is still babes who have not mastered the basics of the first principles of Christ. Not only are they not mature, they are not even toddlers or young adults, but babes. The writer is warning of the danger of not advancing to the point of mature sons and daughters. They are not yet mature enough to discern between good and evil and, therefore, not ready to be a teacher or leader.

The apostle Paul confronted this same immaturity in the church at Corinth (I Cor. 3:1-3). He could not speak to them as spiritual believers but as carnal believers. They were still being led by their flesh and not consistently by the Spirit. As a result, he could not teach them spiritual meat but still gave them the milk of the Word.

"Positioned" as Mature Sons

It's insightful to learn that in Christ's day, when children matured and had been adequately trained, they were "placed" into "sonship." For this important transition, a public ceremony called a *huiothesia* was held.[18] This word literally means "placed as a son." It was different than a *bar mitzvah* ceremony and normally occurred at 30 years of age. The father of the child would invite members of the community to this event, for it was a public announcement that the child was now a fully mature son with full authority to represent the family name and business, giving him a ring, a robe, and sandals. During the ceremony, the father would announce, "You are My beloved Son (*huios)*, in You I am well-pleased." This is why Father God spoke these words at Christ's baptism (Mark 1:11); He was declaring that Christ was fully authorized to speak for Him and conduct His business. It was Christ's *huiothesia*, positioning him as a mature "son."

Isaiah prophesied of Christ, *"For a child will be born to us, a son will be given to us; And the government will rest on His* [the Son's] *shoulders;"* (Is. 9:6). Isaiah later tells us that keys of governmental authority are worn or attached to one's shoulder to lock and unlock, which gives us insight of government keys resting on *"His shoulders"* (see Is. 22:22). Keys of authority on one's shoulder signified "chamberlain authority." Matthew 16:19 tells us that Jesus is, likewise, positioning us as mature sons with chamberlain authority, able to use the keys of kingdom authority to bind and to loose on His behalf.

Huiothesia is usually translated "adoption as sons" in the New Testament (Gal. 4:5; Eph. 1:5). Technically, however, the word isn't saying we are being adopted into God's family. It refers to the above ceremony, stating that as His children, already in the family, we are being positioned or placed into "sonship." Adoption as sons emphasizes spiritual inheritance and identity and applies equally to female as well as male believers. God's

---

[18] Dutch Sheets, *Moving in Greater Authority*, accessed February 13, 2024, https://www.givehim15.com/post/february-13-24

plan is to mature us from spiritual babies to mature sons and daughters, who are qualified to fully represent and speak for Him in our sphere of influence. A fully mature "son" exercises all the rights and privileges of an heir and also possesses *kingdom authority.*

This understanding is important in Romans 8 as well. The chapter tells us that as God's children, we have all the rights, blessings, and privileges of being in His family:

> *"The Spirit Himself testifies with our spirit that we are children* [teknon] *of God, and if children,* [teknon] *heirs also, heirs of God and fellow heirs with Christ, if indeed we suffer with Him so that we may also be glorified with Him"* (Romans 8:16-17, bracket added).

Romans 8 makes an important distinction between children/teenagers (*teknon*) and mature sons, saying that "sons" *(huios*) of God are *led* by His Spirit. *"For all who are being led by the Spirit of God, these are sons (huios) of God"* (Rom. 8:14). Many of God's kids are not yet led by Holy Spirit. Though they have access to His blessings, they are not mature enough to know His voice and ways. Some never grow to this point. Children have rights and benefits; mature sons also possess kingdom authority.

Mature sons also possess kingdom authority.

Paul further writes in Romans 8:

> *For the anxious longing of the creation waits eagerly for the revealing of the sons* [huios] *of God. . .that the creation itself also will be set free from its slavery to corruption into the freedom of the glory of the children of God.* (Romans 8:19, 21, bracket added)

This passage tells us that creation is groaning and travailing, waiting for the revealing of the "sons" of God - NOT the revealing of His children – but the revealing of "sons."

Christians who are at the child level of maturity cannot bring healing to the earth; only mature sons and daughters, those led by Holy Spirit, can do so. These "sons" of God know His Word and ways, carry His heart, and are led by His Spirit, enabling them to represent Christ. There is no better scripture to describe the impact of possessing our communities than the above passage: mature sons setting creation free to reveal the glory of God. As Christ's church, we

Only mature sons and daughters, those led by Holy Spirit, can bring healing to the earth.

are to manifest a level of this sonship now, representing His spiritual authority and releasing His healing to a groaning earth.

Let's Apply!

Do you seek to be led by the Spirit? Are you able to hear His voice?

Are you learning the ways of God as a mature "son?"

The spiritual battle we are a part of has always been between "the sons" -- the sons of light and the sons of darkness. When Jesus was explaining the parable of the tares in Matthew 13, Christ called His disciples "sons of the kingdom" and tares as the "sons of the evil one." Similarly, Paul refers to the battle as between the sons of light and the sons of darkness. The battle is not between the members of the Godhead and the devil, in view of the fact that the devil is our enemy, not God's enemy. No, the battle for our families and communities is between the sons of light and sons of darkness.

A Company of Mature "Sons"

God is maturing a company of believers throughout the earth into their "sonship" stage. He wants you to be a part of this company. God has put guardians and managers in your life to govern you into maturity (Gal. 4:2). Your *guardian* is the Holy Spirit and your *managers* are the fivefold ministers (apostles, prophets, pastors, teachers, and evangelists) who grow you into sonship.

Your guardian is the Holy Spirit and your managers are the fivefold ministers who grow you into sonship.

You are growing in wisdom and knowledge. No longer a spiritual baby or child, you are being matured to a point where you can be trusted with Christ's authority. God gives you a sphere of influence in which you carry his authority to steward for Him in the Kingdom.

As a mature son or daughter, you will bring salvation, healing, and restoration to the needy in your life, teaching them to prosper. Some of you will transform governments, education, economies, medicine, farming, and more. Others of you will be healers of decimated cities and nations (Is. 58:12), delivering the oppressed and downtrodden (Luke 4:18-19). Move in humility, and in power. Operate in love, and release His kingdom authority.

Jesus wants you to be mature and activated as a mature son.

Let's Apply!

God wants to mature you as a son and position you as a mature "son." Are you allowing Him to mature you to take your community?

Let's Internalize and Apply!

1. What does the word *perfection* mean in Hebrews 6:1?

   ____

   ____

2. What does the Greek word *huios* mean?

   ____

   ____

3. What does the Greek term *huiothesia* mean?

   ____

   ____

4. True/False: Adoption as sons emphasizes spiritual inheritance and identity and applies equally to female as well as male believers.

5. True/False: A fully mature "son" exercises all the rights and privileges of an heir and also possesses kingdom authority.

6. True/False: Creation is groaning and travailing, waiting for the revealing of the "sons" of God - NOT the revealing of His "children."

7. The spiritual battle we are a part of has always been between what "sons"?

   ____

   ____

Appendix A: Answers to Internalize & Apply Questions

Chapter 1 – One Version of You

1. The Father only sees you as a new creation in Christ, your new man.
2. Because you are co-identified with Christ, your old nature was left in the grave.
3. The Father only deals with your new man because He killed off your old man on the cross and left it in the grace.

Chapter 2 – Not Modifiable

1. The Father treats you like He treats Jesus.
2. You are seeking to resurrect your old nature that Jesus killed off at the cross. You are responding from your flesh rather than your born-again spirit.
3. Modifying your behavior seeks to modify your old nature. Instead, the Father gave you a new Christ nature and now reprograms your mind with the mind of Christ to reflect the ways of the new man.
4. True.

Chapter 4 – Jesus in the Mirror

1. I AM factor: your I AM-ness from God; how the Father made you and sees you.
2. I Am imposter: an inaccurate understanding of who you are as a Christian.
3. Move to I AM factor by reading God's Word to accurately understand who you are in your born-again spirit, and speak it with your mouth.
4. God the Father has the exclusive right to assign a name to me. I should respond by wearing the name that I have been given from my Creator.

Chapter 5 – What's True About the One Version of You

1. My born-again spirit is the 'real me'.
2. God sees my born-again spirit that is as righteous, holy, perfect, and complete as Jesus. My born-again spirit is as perfect as it will be in eternity.
3. Sin-consciousness: see self as still a sinner at my core; Righteousness consciousness: see self (my identify) as righteous, holy, perfect, and complete as Jesus
4. No, your born-again spirit does not participate in sin and, in fact, is not capable of committing sin.
5. True.
6. True.

Chapter 6: Winning in the Courtroom of Heaven

1. True.
2. The Courts of Heaven are located in the third heaven where God resides.

3. True.
4. True.
5. True.
6. Jesus *judges*, then *makes war*. *Judging* is judicial activity in the courtroom of Heaven (i.e., for us, getting favorable verdicts based upon evidence – repenting and apply the blood of Christ) and *waging war* is battlefield activity (i.e., for us, binding and loosing, declarations, decrees).

Chapter 7: Repenting from Dead Works

1. Dead works is the belief that you can earn the Father's love and acceptance through your human efforts, your good works, or your religious traditions. This leaves you with a *sin-consciousness*.
2. You cleanse your conscience of dead works when you repent of this wrong thinking and ask for the blood of Jesus Christ to speak on your behalf in the Courts.

Chapter 8: The Completeness of Forgiveness

1. No, not an issue between you and God now. God the Father accepted the full payment of His Son on the cross for all your sins – past, present, and future.
2. All my sins – past, present and future – have been forgiven.
3. No. Jesus was offered one time to pay for all my sins – past, present, and the ones I will commit in the future.
4. Heaven. I am righteous and holy in my born-again spirit, and all my sins have been paid for once and for all.

Chapter 9 – The Gift of a Good Conscience

1. Devil, or a defiled (untransformed) conscience
2. Dead works view: that God loves me and accepts me based on my performance – my doing. Your conscience is cleansed from "dead works" when you fully accept that Christ's full payment for your sins is what makes you accepted to the Father.
3. An evil conscience is the erroneous belief that your core self (your spirit) as a Christian is still sinful in some way. It's still thinking that there are two versions of you: your new nature and your old nature. You still have a *sin-consciousness* rather than a *righteousness-consciousness*. You will need to reprogram your conscience by repenting of continuing to believe there are two versions of you and believe the truth that God only sees one version of you – the new man.
4. No, your born-again spirit is as holy, clean, pure, and perfect as Jesus. Your spirit is as perfect and complete as it will ever be.

Chapter 10 – "Give Me Back My Stuff"

1. True.

2. No, negativity is a part of your old man, or sin nature.
3. All of your sins and negativity in all its forms – negative thinking, negative behavior, negative emotions, sarcasm, and cynicism.
4. All negativity is an assault against your identity in Christ, distract from your true identity and destiny, distort how you perceive who you really are in Christ, and challenge the truths God has declared about you.
5. The areas are your *perception* of what's true in your born-again spirit, how you *think* and *feel* about yourself, and how you *talk* about yourself.
6. Attachments come from such sources as the flesh, the world system, and religion.
7. Change the thought to a truth or promise and work on that new thought. Religion tells you to work on the negative thought.
8. True.

Chapter 11: Faith in God

1. God the Father, who is the Judge of all, is for you as He delivered up his Son for you. Jesus is also for you as He died and shed His blood for you. He is also at the right hand of the Father always interceding for you as your advocate and defense attorney.
2. Jesus' shed blood *"speaks better things"* about you in the courts of Heaven and answers every accusation against you.
3. True.
4. First, Christ rescued you from sin by *redeeming* you with His own precious blood. Second, Jesus satisfied the Father's righteous anger, wrath, and fiery indignation against all of your sins and turned aside the Father's wrath forever (known as *propitiation*). As a result of this, the Father is right in *justifying* you.
5. False.
6. True.

Chapter 13: The Recircuiting Process

1. What **lie** am I believing about my identity? What's **true** about my identity?
2. Rejecting and Renouncing the lie followed by Declaring and Announcing what is scripturally true to form a new agreement.

Chapter 14: Becoming a Mature Son

1. The word *perfection* in Hebrews 6:1 means a state of being mature or complete. A fully mature person possesses full authority to represent the family name and business.
2. The Greek word *huios* is a fully matured "son."
3. The term *huiothesia* means "placed" into "sonship." In the case of Christ, the *huiothesia* ceremony positioned him as a mature "son." The Father is telling you, "You are My beloved Son (*huios*), in You I am well-pleased."

4. True.
5. True.
6. True.
7. The spiritual battle we are a part of has always been between "the sons" -- the sons of light and the sons of darkness.

About the Authors

Dr. Lon Stettler is an ordained minister and educator who is very passionate about discipleship and maturity. He has been very active in the discipleship ministry for over four decades. Lon has written, preached, and taught discipleship courses for more than thirty years. He holds a Doctor of Philosophy degree from Miami University in educational leadership and served as a school district administrator for 26 years.

Laurie is a mother of four children and retired high school teacher who enjoys crocheting and time with family. Laurie and Lon have seven wonderful grandchildren.

Lon and Laurie currently live near Charleston, South Carolina.

Contact: lon.stettler@gmail.com or LonStettler.Com

Other books and books by the authors include:

Activating Your True Identity: Learning the Upgrade Principle

Activating the Present-Day Ministry of the Holy Spirit: Activating Saints in the Marketplace

Downloading Heavens Resources: Practical Benefits of Speaking in Tongues

Foundation Stones: 6 Principles to Maturity in Christ

www.ingramcontent.com/pod-product-compliance
Lightning Source LLC
LaVergne TN
LVHW081320110826
845149LV00006B/1550

* 9 7 9 8 9 9 3 6 4 7 8 2 1 *